MW00834249

THE

BEST

ROBOT

IT AIN'T PERSONAL, IT'S JUST BUSINESS

WINS

ISBN: 978-1-954089-65-5   1 2 3 4 5 6 7 8 9 10

Printed in the United States of America

KRYSTAL PARKER

THE BEST ROBOT

IT AIN'T PERSONAL, IT'S JUST BUSINESS

WINS

INSPIRE

CONTENTS

THE

BEST

ROBOT

WINS

INTRODUCTION

With the robot revolution and a push for AI in the workplace, we cannot forget about the inherent value of the human worker. Leaders can gain a competitive advantage when they learn to balance the pendulum between strategy and people. So many people drag themselves to work every day and feel utterly marginalized. In contrast, others take advantage of the fair wage they earn and do not offer the organization value. There is a way to strike a balance between people and processes to edify humans and maximize results.

Business is a machine, and while there are many intricacies required to create a machine, there is a basic formula that, if followed, can produce the best robot. Every business needs systems and processes to support and extract the most outstanding value from its human capital, and every business needs humans to accomplish the mission. Genesis chapter 1 provides a road map for creating a framework so that mankind can thrive. In the beginning, God created the structure first—heavens, earth, light, sky, land, seas, plants, trees, sun, moon, stars, air, and sea creatures—and finally, on day six, He created land animals and mankind. If God were to have created man first, the conditions would have made it impossible to survive. God created the structure, so humankind could thrive.

As a business owner or leader, it is your job to ensure that the structure of your organization aids your human workers in accomplishing the mission. The greater the clarity around systems and processes within the machine the better able you will be to attract, retain, and engage highly qualified and unique human workers to align their purposes and passions toward the mission. By fostering a culture that creates harmony between people and processes, human workers can have fulfilling personal lives and produce results one hundred times greater than the competition.

Many people told me I should reconsider this book's title, make it something softer, easier to understand, more typical, a promise of what people will learn. I was told the title is cold, impersonal; a gut punch that makes no sense and mechanical. Each time someone would look at me funny or even make a face at the title, I celebrated inside! If we are going to impact business culture and help companies transition into this new world, we must be willing to do what others are not doing and pave the way into the future. It is true:

business is a machine. That may seem cold and impersonal, but if the business isn't operating correctly, it doesn't matter how remarkable the talent is in your organization; it will not survive. I need leaders to understand a way to strike a balance between strategy and leadership; it is nonnegotiable. If that seems cold or impersonal to you, I would say, "It ain't personal, it's just business." Several of your own experiences will inevitably bubble to the surface as you read this book. Emotions can drive change, and there has never been a greater need to reconstruct business culture than today. Settle in as you experience the compounding power of people, processes, and parables.

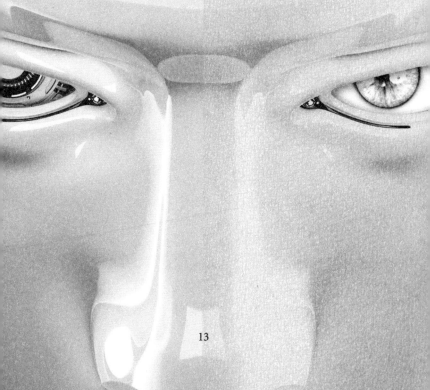

CHAPTER 1

BUSINESS AIN'T PERSONAL— EXCEPT WHEN IT IS

THE

BEST

ROBOT

WINS

f culture eats strategy for breakfast, why are we still hungry?

If strategy were enough, then why are 86 percent of the companies that were on the Fortune 500 list in 1955 no longer in existence today?

If that didn't get your attention, maybe this will: According to Ryan Berman, change consultant and founder of Courageous, "Fifty-two percent of the Fortune 500 companies from the year 2000 are now extinct. That's not a typo. In less than two decades, more than half the brands that were on the Fortune 500 list in 2000 no longer exist."

Consider a global pandemic, rapid change due to digital transformation, and technology evolving at warp speed, then insert a robot revolution—companies that are unable to adapt and adjust rapidly will fail quickly. Just fifty years ago, the life expectancy of a Fortune 500 brand was seventy-five years. Now it's less than fifteen.

Some believe that everything in business rises and falls on leadership, but where is strategy in that approach? This battle between strategy and leadership has been going on as long as Tom has been chasing Jerry.

Encompassing both strategy and leadership are the four basic elements that are the bedrock to business management: planning, leading, organizing, and control. These vintage management principles have improved with big data, lean principles, predictive analytics, and behavioral assessments. However, as good as they get at planning, leading, organizing, and control, companies tend to get lopsided. As a result, there is either greater emphasis on planning and control or leading and organizing.

The age-old power struggle between strategy and leadership creates silos, breaks down communication, and ultimately accelerates a path to failure much more rapidly today than in years past. Take, for example, the speed of execution for Fortune 500 companies. One might ask why. Artificial intelligence and the robot revolution have created a need for an evolution of these vintage management principles and a balance between strategy and leadership.

The world is evolving, and AI is taking over. Robots are vacuuming our floors, assembling and driving our cars, delivering packages, performing customer service, cooking our food, tending to crops, selecting job candidates, becoming our bosses, and transforming the workplace.

NO INDUSTRY IS SAFE FROM AI DISRUPTION.

No industry is safe from AI disruption. We're seeing the impact at every level of our lives from large manufacturing plants "staffed" by machines to offices where power outlets are more important than coffee bars. Even at home, plugins, ports, and fast-speed internet have become a higher priority than closet space. Experts estimate that artificial intelligence and robotics will displace up to seven million jobs between 2017 and 2037. While robots can improve our lives and businesses by reducing costs, improving service, and taking over repetitive tasks, employers are having difficulty disaggregating the treatment of humans with robots. At the same time, because of this "robot revolution," humans are feeling increasingly disenfranchised and often displaced and disengaged from the company's mission.

EXPERTS ESTIMATE THAT ARTIFICIAL INTELLIGENCE AND ROBOTICS WILL DISPLACE UP TO SEVEN MILLION JOBS BETWEEN 2017 AND 2037.

How many times have you been told to leave your personal life at the door when you walk into work? This isn't a new management attitude, but AI is exacerbating it. "Separate your personal and professional lives," a mentor once told me. If no one has ever told you that, you've probably at least heard the saying *take off your personal hat and put on your company hat*. And then there's my favorite: *it ain't personal, it's just business*.

The companies that will survive into the twenty-first century are the ones that recognize, respect, and respond to the dichotomy of humans and robots. The leaders of those organizations value and care about people even as they attempt to maximize results with technology.

I left corporate America after fifteen years of climbing the executive ladder. I had become vanilla, blending in to fit the mold, doing what was expected, wearing my company hat so much that I didn't know who I was outside of work. I was a shell of a human with an identity crisis. I'd even figured out how to do that with my faith. I was a Sunday Christian, attending church every week but leaving the message behind when I walked out the door.

My daughter was five years old at the time. When I told her I no longer worked for the company I'd spent so many years with, she cried. Through her tears, she said, "But you're Krystal Parker, vice president. Who will you be now?"

I didn't know. Even worse, I had been so busy trying to figure it out that I ignored the bigger issue: the child who should have known me as *mom* had come to know me better as *executive*. My identity was wrapped up so tightly in the company I served that, without my job, I was empty with no real understanding of my true identity or purpose in life. Who was I other than Krystal Parker, executive?

Is it possible for a person to find his or her purpose, have a fulfilling personal life, and still contribute to the organization? I believe the answer is yes. Even more, it's vital for an organization to employ, encourage, and foster a culture that inspires people to experience alignment between purpose and vocation to contribute at a higher ratio.

It's imperative that leaders understand *who* is pulling the levers in the organization instead of *what* is pulling the levers. Employers must recognize the contributions humans make and understand that robots and humans can't be managed the same because they're not the same.

I have a Roomba® and I can't tell you how many times that machine gets into trouble by getting stuck or off-balance or even misses a spot I want it to vacuum. Sometimes I have to stand over it, so it vacuums exactly where I want it to. This is a silly example to illustrate that when you have a structure in place, the machine can be improved with human intervention. Humans are and will continue to be required no matter how advanced technology is. Their role may change, but the need for them won't.

While vital, technology alone is not enough. Organizations need to balance the investments of human capital and technology— and it's not easy. Companies I work with are either winning with technology and losing with their human workforce, or they're winning with people and neglecting to innovate through the use of technology. Herein lies the opposition between strategy and leadership.

Gartner, the world's leading research and advisory company, "predicts tech spending for 2021 to be $3.9 trillion, a 6.2 percent increase from 2020." Gartner also expects legal tech spending to increase 200 percent by 2025, and IT spending in organizations will continue to rise. Automation software is getting a big boost in spending, "with plenty of CIOs predicting they are likely to double the number of software 'bots' they are using to increase productivity" and reduce reliance on human workers. Gartner research also reveals that the vast majority of IT and business leaders say that the most important skills needed over the next ten years will be soft skills—people skills, communication skills, social skills, and other personal attributes that enable us to work effectively and harmoniously with others. No matter how far technology advances, this truth remains: over the past century, soft skills have been the best predictor of success in business.

My dad once told me, "Krystal, you are not as smart as your brother and sister. You will need to luck into a good job." Indeed, book smarts did not come easily to me. There were countless nights I would be up studying at the kitchen table past midnight to pass a test the next day. What did come easily and natural to me was people skills—that's where I excelled. Research conducted by Harvard University, the Carnegie Foundation, and Stanford Research Center all concluded that 85 percent of job success comes from having well-developed soft and people skills, leaving 15 percent of job success credited to technical skills and knowledge.

As important as technology is, a soft-skills deficit creates significant opportunity costs for organizations. Companies that invest in human capital and reskilling the workforce will strengthen leaders, reduce turnover, improve efficiency, and adapt to change more quickly. The pendulum shouldn't swing too far left or right—it's vital to balance technology and people. Doing that will position your company for longevity, success, and overall domination of the competition.

Where Is the Real Value?

When I was thirty-four and relatively new in my role as a corporate officer, I was responsible for running the gas company in forty-seven cities along the west side of Texas. I was in a meeting with my supervisor and peers discussing our investment strategy for the upcoming budget year. In response to the pushback I was getting on my proposed training budget, I said, "Yes, I understand we are in fact standing on over $300 million of pipeline, but our greatest asset is our human capital." At first, it got so quiet I could hear the second hand ticking on the clock—and then the laughter drowned out the sound of the clock.

I could feel the blood pumping from my heart directly to my face. As I blushed, I remembered what my dad said about not being very smart. Thankfully, they laughed long enough for me to remember everything I'd accomplished. I didn't go from being a college dropout stocking shelves in a dusty old truck parts store to the youngest vice president in this Fortune 500 company's history by believing infrastructure had more value than people. I knew that some leaders valued pipe, technology, and machines more than they valued people. I also knew they were wrong.

Regardless of the industry, humans are every organization's greatest asset. John Maxwell says, "People determine the potential in your organization." He's right! That's why leaders must remember that human workers are individuals with personal lives, feelings, experiences, values, creativity, and—ultimately—intellectual capital.

General Norman Schwarzkopf said it this way: "I have seen competent leaders who stood in front of a platoon and all they saw was a platoon. But great leaders stand in front of a platoon and see it as forty-four individuals, each of whom has aspirations, each of whom wants to live, each of whom wants to do good." Yes, AI and the robot revolution are important. However, the ones pulling the levers, creating the robots, innovating, adapting to customers, and solving complex problems are the humans working in your organization.

It is not uncommon to hear employees talk about work documents as their "training bible" or their "company bible." Every office should be equipped with the greatest business book ever written: the Holy Bible.

The Bible has so much to say about business. We're going to focus on two key lessons: one, the Parable of the Sower, which explains the importance of creating an environment in which your people can grow and thrive and two, the Parable of the Talents, which helps every person from CEO to individual worker understand the importance of their unique contributions. Rich, rewarding, wonderful workplaces that spark, motivate, and inspire humans do not happen by accident nor do they always equate to companies standing the test of time. Processes and systems do not have to suffocate rich, rewarding workplaces. However, if the company is not profitable, the company will cease to exist. *It ain't personal, it's just business.*

It's vital we align individuals' contributions and skill sets with the overall corporate mission because the human worker will never be extinct. The consulting firm PwC estimates that between 2017 and 2037 "the reduction in costs caused by the use of AI and robots would, in turn, generate *7.2 million new jobs*, giving a net gain of *200,000 jobs*." Think about it: if the human worker will always be around, how much more will your organization be improved by structuring your company to reskill and retrain the human capital? Replacement costs can range from one-half to two times the employee's annual salary.

Gartner research shows that the most admired leadership trait is transparency, followed by authentic communications and collaboration. CIOs ranked above average are more likely to develop others through coaching and mentoring than low-performing

CIOs (69 percent vs. 48 percent). In a one-to-one setting with their direct reports, high-performing CIOs say that up to 74 percent of their time is spent listening rather than directing.

||||||||||||||||||||||||||||||||||||||||||||||||||||||||||||||||||||||||||||||||||||||||||||||||||||||||

IT'S VITAL WE ALIGN INDIVIDUALS' CONTRIBUTIONS AND SKILL SETS WITH THE OVERALL CORPORATE MISSION BECAUSE THE HUMAN WORKER WILL NEVER BE EXTINCT.

||||||||||||||||||||||||||||||||||||||||||||||||||||||||||||||||||||||||||||||||||||||||||||||||||||||||

The way to create a culture that allows leaders to lead effectively is to create an environment that provides people with systems and processes that marry their roles with the organization's goals, empowering people to be successful. So, for example, instead of following my Roomba around, let's say I lean into technology, set up invisible parameters, safeguard the areas where it gets stuck, and help my Roomba successfully do its job. By doing this, I don't have to micromanage my Roomba, and I can focus on *my* job.

When I visualize business, I see it as a machine made up of several parts, gears, and axles working together to power something (or create power). If you break down a business piece by piece, you find people, processes, and systems. When those three things are working in conjunction, operations are flowing very well. When they're out of alignment or the wrong systems, processes, or people are in place, it can create friction and often disrupt or destroy the workflow.

Imagine two hamsters running on separate wheels. One wheel is in alignment, turning perfectly; the other wheel is out of alignment, distorted, barely turning. Which hamster will be able to run faster?

The idea is to set up the correct processes and systems to enable your workforce to run and adapt more quickly. For a company to be more effective and create a competitive advantage, systems and processes need to be established that will help your people excel in the roles they play within your organization.

The business landscape is brutal, and the engine must be running at peak performance to power the machine.

Begin with the Foundation

Not long ago, a construction company was doing some building in my neighborhood. They would work and work, day after day, getting the foundation just right and then all of a sudden there would be a house standing. It took much more time to get the foundation set correctly with the adequate infrastructure than to erect the actual home.

When I think of creating the correct systems and processes for employees to be successful, it reminds me of one of the teachings that Jesus shared during the Sermon on the Mount about the Parable of the Wise and Foolish Builders:

> *Therefore, everyone who hears these words of mine and puts them into practice is like a wise man who built his house on the rock. The rain came down, the streams rose, and the winds blew and beat against that house; yet it did not fall, because it had its foundation on the rock. But everyone who hears these words of mine and does not put them into practice is like a foolish man who built his house on sand. The rain came down, the streams rose, and the winds blew and beat against that house, and it fell with a great crash.*
> —Matthew 7:24-27 (NIV)

The rock illustrates the importance of building one's life on the foundation of Jesus Christ. This lesson also reinforces the importance of having that strong foundation in the workplace.

The Parable of the Sower teaches us the importance of environment. In Chapter 3, we'll begin our discussion of how that lesson can help leaders understand that by using systems and processes correctly to structure the right environment, they can extract the greatest amount of value from the people working in the organization. When that happens, Fortune 500 leaders, small business owners, nonprofits, and volunteer organizations can expect to improve service standards, reduce turnover which leads to a reduction in operating costs, increase output, and most importantly create a workforce that is—hold please, I just heard my Roomba say, "Error. Please move Roomba to a new location."

I'm back. Where was I? Oh! And most importantly, create a workforce that's working together to innovate, adapt, evolve, grow, and ultimately stand the test of time.

CHAPTER 2

THE ART AND SCIENCE OF THE MANAGEMENT MACHINE

THE

BEST

ROBOT

WINS

A n efficient management machine is a balanced blend of art and science. The best-performing companies find harmony between measurement and meaning. The better the machine is constructed, the more effective you will be at serving your customer. I visualize a pendulum swinging back and forth between strategy and leadership, and ultimately that pendulum should rest in the middle. The best way to accomplish this is to create harmony between the vintage management principles which encompass both the art and science of management. The art, which is organizing and leading people, can be improved with sound science, which includes planning and controls within the organization.

Pastor and leadership expert Craig Groeschel says, "Your life will always move in the direction of your strongest thoughts." Substitute the word *business* for *life,* and the statement remains true. Your business will always move in the direction of your strongest thoughts. Think of it like a ship's rudder. James 3:4 (NIV) instructs, ". . . Take ships as an example. Although they are so large and are driven by strong winds, they are steered by a very small rudder wherever the pilot wants to go."

Something as small and invisible as a thought can impact the entire organization, which is why understanding behavioral science is essential to constructing your management machine.

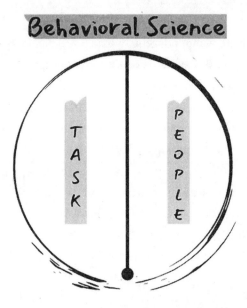

Let's break this down: Behavioral science teaches us that humans are either more task-oriented or more people-oriented. These orientations are not mutually exclusive. It's not that task-oriented individuals don't care about people or that people-oriented individuals can't complete tasks, but we all lean one way or the other. And there's nothing wrong with being either way. In fact, both orientations are strengths in their own ways. But any strength out of control can become a weakness, which is why understanding and balance are so essential.

As the term indicates, task-oriented people are more concerned about completing tasks than building relationships with people. You might hear these individuals say, "Process over people," or, as in the story I shared in Chapter 1 about the corporate officers being so amused by my insistence that people were our greatest asset, they place more value on infrastructure than humans. Task-oriented individuals enjoy and prefer strategy, numbers, and metrics over human interactions.

When structuring or leading an organization, a task-oriented individual will likely have firm controls and processes in place. Approval procedures, work schedules, and goals are transactional and process-driven. These leaders place a tremendous amount of performance value on metrics and numbers. The value a task-oriented leader brings to the organization is an ability to manage and measure progress, mitigate risk, create structure, and keep the gears turning.

But too much of a good thing can be bad for you. As it says in Proverbs, "If you find honey, eat just enough—too much of it, and you will vomit" (Proverbs 25:16, NIV). In a business, too much of one orientation can lead to other factors being neglected.

An organization run with a strong task orientation can become too mechanical. Too much focus on process, task management, and measurement can slow down the machine, quell creativity and innovation, and increase turnover. That, in turn, reduces the ability of the organization to adapt and grow.

When leaders only care to look at the black and white numbers, they place more value on metrics than individuals. As a result, it's not uncommon to hear a task-oriented leader say, "It ain't personal, it's just business," or "Don't do for one that which you can't do for a hundred." They may even think that if a person is producing well, they should give that person more work, completely neglecting the need for work-life balance or job fulfillment.

During the pandemic, I had a conversation with a manager who had taken on the work of two eliminated positions in her company. She was working as hard as she could, and she was exhausted. She said, "I have come to the conclusion that if I died today, come tomorrow, someone would be sitting in my chair. Krystal, I'm just a number. They don't care about me as a human being. As long as I perform, they pile more and more on me. Once I am gone, someone else will take my spot, and they won't miss a beat." Her feelings are far from unique in the corporate world.

She agreed to let me use her quote but asked to remain anonymous. The fact that she didn't want me to identify her or her company speaks volumes about her lack of trust in the organization. In organizations heavy on task orientation, people become a byproduct. As long as they produce, they remain in the machine. When they stop producing, they're gone. Treating people as a byproduct will not yield the maximum amount of value from your talent. When employees are engaged, motivated, and committed to the overall mission, they produce higher returns, creating a multiplier effect. The Parable of the Sower we'll begin discussing in Chapter 3 will demonstrate how to structure your organization to gain maximum value from your human capital.

On the other side of the equation are the people-oriented individuals. You might hear them say, "People over process." These leaders are more focused on people and quality relationships. They manage with intuition and feelings rather than structure and numbers. They know personal stories about each individual who works for them. People-oriented leaders are usually loved by the people in the organization. They're great with change management and getting buy-in from the workforce. They create environments that are fun, inspirational, and filled with rewards. They celebrate human successes and create happy, motivated employees.

When the strength of being people-oriented is out of control, we often see a lack of accountability, measurements, and control. Those leaders tend to avoid conflict and place personal relationships over doing what is best for the organization. People-oriented individuals can allow their personal connections with employees to put the mission at risk. People-orientation without necessary processes can cause a company to function irresponsibly. It's not uncommon to hear a people-oriented leader say, "Do for one that which you cannot do for a hundred."

Figuring This Out in the Real World

Imagine a psychology major working in the oil and gas industry surrounded by a sea of engineers. Engineers typically lean more toward process over people and relationships. I, on the other hand, leaned more toward people over process.

This was especially true early in my career. I had dropped out of college with just twenty-one credits needed for a degree. I returned to my small hometown and began my career stocking shelves in a truck parts store that was a subsidiary of the gas company. The store was a pilot program that didn't work out. I had been doing a good job at secretarial work, so instead of being laid off when the store closed, I was offered a job as the front desk secretary for a gas-gathering team about thirty miles away. Not long after that, the bookkeeper in that office left, and I took on that role in addition to my secretarial duties. I didn't know anything about accounting, but I learned. I enjoyed most of my work and was able to buy my first house.

Life was pretty good, but I wanted more—more growth, more responsibility, more money. When I finally got the courage to ask my manager what it would take to move up in the organization, he looked at me with a puzzled expression and said, "You'll have to move to another area in the company and take an office job. Maybe something in HR." He wasn't being mean, but he couldn't believe I could ever be a field supervisor or lead a team of field workers. I was the only female in the office, and he only saw me as an office administrative worker.

I took his advice and applied for an HR job in a division office for one of the distribution companies six and a half hours away.

Three senior executives—two women and one man—conducted the interview. One was Glenda, the HR director who would become my first professional mentor, and a man and a woman who didn't say their titles when they introduced themselves. This was the natural gas distribution side of the business, and I worked for the partners. I was unfamiliar with the natural gas distribution companies but getting a quick education. During the interview, the woman said, "Name two vice presidents for Kansas Gas Service."

Taking a deep breath, I named three vice presidents on the corporation's partners' side, giving her the two she asked for and an extra for good measure. Then I said, "I apologize. I don't know any on the distribution side of the business."

She looked over the top of her glasses and said, "Well, you're looking at two right now."

I maintained my composure despite my embarrassment—and excitement. There was a woman officer, a woman who was a boss over field employees.

As I was processing this, it hit me: if two vice presidents and the HR director were in the room for this interview, it must be an important job. I hadn't thought much about that before. I had just found an opening that seemed to fit my manager's advice for how to get promoted. And I was too naïve to understand that I should be intimidated by these senior officers.

I got the job and went to work for Glenda, who was the first person in the company to recognize my potential. She encouraged me to go back to school, finish those lingering twenty-one credit hours, and get my degree in psychology. It ended up taking me a total of ten years to get that first degree, but that was part of my journey.

I'll never forget the day I graduated. Glenda met me at Borders bookstore, where she gave me a copy of *Secrets of Six-Figure*

Women by Barbara Stanny and a bottle of wine. The wine came and went, but the book stuck with me forever. Stanny's primary message was to do what you're passionate about and you'll be successful.

At the time, I was barely making $30,000 a year. To think Glenda believed that one day I might actually make six figures was mind-blowing. I never envisioned that for myself. I don't even know if it was what was in the book that was so powerful or if it was the fact that someone I looked up to believed that I was worth six figures and was giving me the step-by-step instructions to get there one day.

Another piece of advice Glenda gave me was that I needed super-visory experience if I was going to move up in the company. Even though I bragged about my management experience from my job at my hometown swimming pool, she wasn't impressed. Not long after telling me that, she was moved out of HR and into the position of director over customer service for the entire state of Kansas. There were two openings in the union call center for supervisors—positions typically filled from within and that happened to fall two levels below her new role.

So even though I didn't know anything about the systems, the regulatory environment, or what I was getting into, I applied for one of those jobs. With the support of my former boss, I became a supervisor, and it didn't take me long to figure out what I'd gotten into. I was in my mid-twenties supervising long-time union employees, many of whom were my parents' age. At the time, there were a lot of grievances. With the former director of HR becoming the director of customer service and an HR generalist coming in as a supervisor, the workers thought I was a spy, so you can imagine how they treated me. To add to my challenges, my peer supervisors were not at all impressed with me. They had come up through the customer service ranks and saw no value in what I brought to the job. My new boss, the customer service manager, made it quite clear that I wouldn't have gotten the job if there hadn't been two openings. The proverbial icing on the cake was that many of the customer service employees hated their jobs, but the pay was good and there were no comparable opportunities that would allow them to earn the same and do something they enjoyed. We were all working in a pressure cooker.

A call center is a heavily measured business and very challenging work. In our efforts to deliver exceptional service, we monitored business performance by analyzing key performance indicators. The idea was to see how we were doing in the present and identify and leverage opportunities for future process improvement. Those customer service and billing key performance indicators included answered call rate, average speed of answer, average handle time, workforce management index, workforce commitment, first call resolution, quality assurance score, web average turnaround time, and more. In other words, we knew the loaded labor cost per second. In fact, we knew every breath these agents took and how much money it cost the company.

As a people-oriented individual walking into an environment where priority is placed on process, this was my first real awareness of the need to balance the pendulum. Strong measurement and control without leadership creates a hostile work environment. Now I understood all the grievances coming from the call center. To address some of those issues, I advocated for holding team meetings but was told we don't take the agents off the phones for meetings. I persisted, presented my agenda, and eventually got approval to meet with my team off the phones for exactly one hour. This eventually became a monthly practice at the call center for each of the teams.

Measurement is a great tool, but it's not enough to give employees a sense of community, belonging, and fulfillment. Too much emphasis on measurement without a balanced concern for people creates a stressful work environment that negatively impacts performance. Negativity in the workplace creates a vicious cycle of stress that impacts employee attendance, performance, work effort, and service levels. As you can see from the chart on page 42, job stress costs American companies more than $300 billion a year in health costs, absenteeism, and poor performance.

||||||||||||||||||||||||||||||||||||||||||||||||||||||||||||||||||||||||||||||||||||||||||||||

MEASUREMENT IS A GREAT TOOL, BUT IT'S NOT ENOUGH TO GIVE EMPLOYEES A SENSE OF COMMUNITY, BELONGING, AND FULFILLMENT.

||||||||||||||||||||||||||||||||||||||||||||||||||||||||||||||||||||||||||||||||||||||||||||||

Table 1: Impacts of a Negative Workplace Environment			
48%	Intentionally decreased their work effort	66%	Said that their performance declined
47%	Intentionally decreased the time spent at their work	78%	Said that their commitment to the organization declined
38%	Intentionally decreased the quality of their work.	12%	Said that they left their job because of the uncivil treatment
80%	Lost work time worrying about the incident	25%	Admitted to taking their frustration out on customers.
63%	Lost work time avoiding the offender		

This table retrieved from the U.S. Chamber Foundation, shows the impact of a negative work environment on an employee's behavior.

In the beginning, there were many days I would practically run to my car and cry for fifteen of the fifty minutes it took to drive home from work. If the employees were not mean to me, I was stressed and frustrated by the management practices I had to follow that were so outside of my comfort zone. For example, there was an elevated platform in the middle of the call center called TIM (Thing In the Middle). The job of the "lucky" supervisor that day was to monitor the employees from that platform to see if they were not ready for calls or on a call too long. The idea was to identify problems and address them, but the employees didn't see it that way. This lucky supervisor was also the one to answer technical questions, take calls from irate customers, and generally manage the floor operation.

The days that I was the supervisor on TIM were especially brutal for me because I didn't know the regulatory rules or the CIS system. I had customers screaming at me and crying to me, begging to get their gas turned back on for a hot shower or a warm home. Employees were taking advantage of me by not logging in to take calls, and I could see the call queue building with callers waiting for a customer service agent. As a regulated industry, we were subject to fines if we did not answer a minimum percentage of calls. If someone hung up in our call queue while waiting for an agent to take their call, it would be considered an abandoned call. If the number of abandoned calls reached a certain threshold for the year, we would be charged an unbudgeted $750,000 penalty. The pressure to perform was unbelievable.

This tough work environment was so far outside of my natural orientation of people leadership that I was miserable. My choices were to quit or change things—and I'm not a quitter. So, I decided to do something different. I would follow my strongest impulse, my natural inclination, which was to connect with people. I would get to know the employees who reported to me and learn their job.

Each agent's workstation included a headset outlet that let someone else come up next to them and plug into the call they were on. Usually, this tool was used when a new hire was sitting with an experienced customer service agent for training and mentoring, but it was the best way for me to experience what they went through and learn the language of the job.

I came out of my office, grabbed a headset, and plugged in with every single one of my agents. As I shared their experiences, I neglected my email duties and the very coveted need to look super important in my office. It was worth it.

Sitting next to each member of my team, I was able to see their personal pictures and mementos, ask questions about their home and families, and learn what they liked to do outside of work. Suddenly, these robots became human. And when they became human to me, I became a leader to them.

You've probably heard all the famous John Maxwell sayings:

People don't care how much you know until they know how much you care.

Always touch a person's heart before you ask him for a hand.

To lead yourself, use your head. To lead others, use your heart.

Every one of those sayings is true.

Once I applied what came naturally to me, the ice started to melt. I found my stride as a supervisor and started to advocate for the members of my team. I pushed for meetings, training, and side-by-side development. I connected with a supervisor who had the exact opposite of my skill set. She was great with the policies and procedures. She knew the ropes, the system, and all of the ins and outs. She saw value in what I was doing. I was able to see the brilliance in her leadership style, and together we started helping each other. I went from being the "idiot in the middle" to a leader they respected. But even as I leaned on my ability to connect with people through my people orientation, I started to understand the value of task orientation and the need to keep the balance. I understood that while I could not be all things, I could be my best me, align myself with great people who had skill sets different from mine, and we could go further together.

The environment of the call center when I started there is a great example of what can happen when the pendulum swings too far to one side. I had to immerse myself in metrics, which let me see firsthand the managing power of measurement. In my three years as a supervisor, I learned the benefits of combining art and science for management. Once I was able to connect with each person on the team, gain their trust, and help them be successful in this heavily measured environment, the team really shined. My time as a call center supervisor went from being one of the most difficult to one of the most rewarding and important lessons in my career.

I understand now that my pendulum swung too far toward people orientation. Without measurement and controls, I was an ineffective leader. At the same time, I learned that highly measured and monitored workplaces without a people-oriented leader involved can become too mechanical. When the pendulum rests in the middle and there is a balance of task- and people-orientation, leaders can capitalize on the multiplier effect and yield higher returns on human capital investment. Having a clear understanding of this is essential when forming a team.

Neither side of this equation is right or wrong; both types of people are needed to create the machine. But what ends up happening is like attracts like and, without attention to this, over time, the scale will become unbalanced and tip one way or the other. Leaders with a people orientation will flock toward leaders with people orientation; leaders that value task will oftentimes hire task-oriented people. I see this firsthand when consulting with companies and boards. Leaders are drawn to individuals with traits that are most like them. This speaks to inherent and acquired diversity traits. When leaders are unaware of the implicit biases around hiring, they will unknowingly fill their team or organization with individuals who profile very close to them.

It's vital for an organization to use measurements and controls to help their employees be successful in their jobs but not at the expense of removing their ability to feel that they matter as humans. Managing with art and science creates a balanced team of task- and people-oriented individuals. This can create the multiplier effect and maximize the returns of people, processes, and systems all working together. Applying this concept when building a team may even mean passing on a candidate that is most like you and going with a qualified candidate that makes you feel a little uncomfortable. You just have to remember: *it ain't personal, it's just business.*

IT'S VITAL FOR AN ORGANIZATION TO USE MEASUREMENTS AND CONTROLS TO HELP THEIR EMPLOYEES BE SUCCESSFUL IN THEIR JOBS BUT NOT AT THE EXPENSE OF REMOVING THEIR ABILITY TO FEEL THAT THEY MATTER AS HUMANS.

The answer to creating this balance in your organization is hiding in plain sight within the Parable of the Sower, spoken by the greatest leader of all time, Jesus of Nazareth. While the parable was recorded more than two thousand years ago, I challenge you to apply it to your business today and watch the power of the competitive advantage it delivers.

CHAPTER 3

SOWING THE SEEDS

THE

BEST

ROBOT

WINS

You've probably heard people refer to their company manual as the operations bible, the employee bible, or something similar. Organizations that call their holy grail for operations the company bible have one thing right: The Holy Bible is *the* operating manual for all things. The Holy Bible is the instruction manual for life—all of it, including business. When you take business principles based on biblical lessons and apply them to every situation, the practical wisdom is infinite.

Let's take the Parable of the Sower, for example. It appears in Matthew, Mark, and Luke. Jesus is speaking to a crowd and He shares this story:

> *A farmer went out to sow his seed. As he was scattering the seed, some fell along the path; it was trampled on, and the birds ate it up. Some fell on rocky ground, and when it came up, the plants withered because they had no moisture. Other seed fell among thorns, which grew up with it and choked the plants. Still other seed fell on good soil. It came up*

and yielded a crop, a hundred times more than was
sown. —Luke 8:5-8 (NIV)

Jesus later explains the soil is a reference to your heart and the seed represents the Word of God. The foundational principles of this parable are not only right; they can also be applied to many business examples around employee and customer retention. You can apply this parable when creating an organizational machine that will extract maximum value from your human and intellectual capital.

REMEMBER, BUSINESS IS A MACHINE, AND WHEN YOU BREAK IT DOWN, YOU FIND PEOPLE, PROCESSES, AND SYSTEMS (PARTS, GEARS, AND AXLES) ALL WORKING TOGETHER TO POWER SOMETHING OR CREATE POWER.

Remember, business is a machine, and when you break it down, you find people, processes, and systems (parts, gears, and axles) all working together to power something or create power. When you apply this parable to your organization, the seed represents your people, and the soil is your processes and systems. Your goal is to create processes and systems that will maximize the value of your workforce—in some cases, by as much as one hundred times.

> *Still other seed fell on good soil. It came up, grew and produced a crop, some multiplying thirty, some sixty, some a hundred times. —Mark 4:8 (NIV)*

You'll gain a tremendous competitive advantage by implementing the lessons from the Parable of the Sower. You'll be able to:

- Attract and retain top talent.
- Increase customer retention.
- Generate higher returns through employee engagement and development.
- Reduce operating costs.
- Enhance customer service.
- Improve communication.
- Simplify and streamline at every level.
- Decrease safety incidents.
- Adapt to a rapidly changing business landscape.
- Create a culture that will outpace and outlast the competition.

Let's start with the first point in the Parable of the Sower:

PARABLE OF THE SEED SOWER

The Path   **The Rocks**   **Thorns**   **Good Soil**

> *Listen! A farmer went out to sow his seed. As he was*
> *scattering the seed, some fell along the path, and the*
> *birds came and ate it up. —Mark 4:3-4 (NIV)*

The seed the birds ate represents your employees who are not plugged in or engaged. They fell along the path and never took root. Don't waste the potential of people who could be excellent if they were planted in the right soil. Learn how to identify and provide the soil your people need.

Managing humans has come down to a set of data points. Companies are creating predictive analytics designed to forecast human behavior for a number of areas inherent to their business, such as retention, engagement, health, job satisfaction, performance, and more. It's not a surprise that, in most cases, your workforce is your greatest asset and highest expense. With predictive analytics, employers are racing to find unique data sets that best predict employee engagement. Companies that utilize analytics to manage and predict human behavior are able to create programs that retain and engage their human talent and, in return, gain a decisive edge in the market.

There is a direct link from employee engagement to your top-line and bottom-line revenues. It's proven that happy, healthy employees create satisfied, returning customers and give any organization a competitive advantage. According to *Harvard Business Review*, Best Buy found that if they can increase employee engagement by 0.1 percent, the value is equivalent to a $100,000 increase in revenue at a single store. So you don't miss this, I am going to break it down:

(SS = Single Store | EE = Employee Engagement | EV = Equivalent Value)

Best Buy: SS + 0.1% EE = $100,000 EV

In its *State of American Workplace* report, Gallup found the more engaged businesses showed:

- 41 percent less absenteeism
- 24-59 percent less turnover
- 28 percent less shrinkage
- 70 percent fewer safety incidents

- 17 percent greater productivity
- 21 percent higher profitability

Employees not engaged or ingrained in your organization are like seeds scattered on the ground—they can easily be blown around by the wind. Individuals who are not mentally and emotionally present or plugged in easily fall away from the mission and increase costs to your organization. Developing employee engagement begins on day one.

In many organizations, a typical first day for a new employee involves showing them their desk and the restrooms and giving them the four Ps: password, paperwork, processes, and a project. The expectation is that the employee knows exactly what to do and how to do it. Whether they do or don't is not the point. The point is that the four Ps will not create employee engagement.

Business trailblazers like the late Tony Hsieh understand the importance of employee engagement and retaining the right talent. Hsieh pioneered a practice of offering employees a quitting bonus. New employees who aren't happy or don't feel like they can handle the work can walk away with $2,000. Imagine creating a culture in which you offer an employee $2,000 to leave in their first four weeks, and they pass it up for the opportunity to work at your company!

The watercooler, aka the breakroom, is where employees learn about the culture, values, and ways to behave and survive within the organization. The stories shared inside the walls of your organization make up the largest and most impactful amount of onboarding experience your new hires will experience. Organizational tales become your culture, and changing the culture means changing the narrative when the leader is not around.

When I consult with a company, I like to spend time with front-line employees and supervisors listening to stories about the organization. Regardless of the signs on the wall or the fancy boilerplate messages you have posted on your website, these real-life stories are what make up the culture and the truth about your organization.

In today's information-age world, employees rank and review workplaces, just as customers review products, services, and companies. No matter how much advertising a company does to sell a product, if the reviews are bad, sales will also be bad. Employees are picking companies based on reviews, just as customers are making purchasing decisions based on reviews. Creating a strong organizational culture that engages people and customers is the first step to attracting, developing, and retaining top talent.

CREATING A STRONG ORGANIZATIONAL CULTURE THAT ENGAGES PEOPLE AND CUSTOMERS IS THE FIRST STEP TO ATTRACTING, DEVELOPING, AND RETAINING TOP TALENT.

That's important because companies that can attract, develop, and retain top talent have a competitive advantage. Regardless of the amount of time you spend creating PowerPoint presentations and company slogans, employees learn the most about the company and how to operate within the company by watching and listening to their peers and leaders. More is caught than taught in an organization.

I had been the vice president in El Paso for a couple of years, responsible for gas operations out of that city. One of my directors told me a story that reinforced this concept of creating a strong organizational culture.

A potential new hire from outside the company had applied for a service person position several times. Each time he was turned down because he needed to speak a little more English for the customer-facing job he wanted. So, he would enroll in programs to improve his English and apply again. Over several years, he repeatedly applied for and didn't get the job he wanted. Finally, the hiring supervisor said to him, "This is your fifth time to interview with us. Why do you keep coming back?"

With a serious expression on his face and emotion in his eyes, he pointed to a man wearing one of our branded logo polos and said, "I want to have that on my chest." He was more than qualified for the job, he was driven to be a part of the organization, he showed perseverance and dedication and, once he was able to demonstrate he could service the English-speaking customers, he was hired and started the service school.

To show you the importance of culture and stories, the hiring supervisor told the manager, the manager shared this with the director, and the director found it important enough to share with me. This was the type of story that was important in the organizational culture we established. Typically, we did not give the new hires our logo shirts until they passed service school and got through the mentoring program. My director went on to say, "Our new hire's cousin works for the company and is letting him borrow his uniforms while he is in service school."

I left my office, walked across the yard, and entered service school. It was easy to spot the only trainee wearing one of our shirts. After welcoming the entire class, I made a point to introduce myself to him. With a firm handshake, looking directly into his eyes, I said, "I heard the story about how hard you worked to get this job. I wanted to come and personally welcome you to the team." I will never forget the smile I received in exchange. I'm not quite sure how much English he actually spoke, but I was thrilled to have him on our team because of how much he wanted to be there.

Though a strong organizational culture and competitive salary, benefits, and life work programs can help you attract the right seed into your company, retention efforts are vital. You work hard to attract the right employees (seed), and you want to get the seed in the ground as quickly as possible. However, in the absence of a strategic orientation process, you are leaving your "seed" or people to chance, or, as Luke wrote, to be trampled on or eaten by the birds.

Given that stories make up a significant portion of the onboarding process, and employees are likely to listen to one another over boilerplate messages by the company, you should create a strategic onboarding team. In the example above, the onboarding with the new hire was already being done by his cousin, who was a tremendous asset to the organization. When culture is strong, effective orientation is simplified. Comprise your orientation team of peer employees who demonstrate the character, attitude, work ethic, and performance you would like new employees to emulate.

Companies with strategic onboarding and orientation processes enjoy higher retention rates. Research by Glassdoor found that organizations with a robust onboarding process improve new hire retention by 82 percent and productivity by over 70 percent. You cannot afford to leave this process to chance. In the absence of a systematic approach to onboarding, you risk your valuable seed falling along the path where it won't take root. Every supervisor and department manager will have their own unique style and approach. Some will do it great, and others will not understand why someone needs more than the four Ps to get started. Create an effective onboarding process, teach your supervisors and managers how to implement it, and measure how they do it.

In addition to the lost opportunity costs related to not getting the seed in rich soil, there are hard dollar costs. The Society for Human Resource Management (SHRM) reports that, on average, it costs the equivalent of six to nine months of an employee's salary to replace them. For an employee making $60,000 per year, that comes out to $30,000-$45,000 in recruiting and training costs, and it's nearly impossible to calculate the lost opportunity costs. This can equate to millions of dollars in actual expenses to an organization plus the cost of not utilizing the human and intellectual capital quickly and effectively.

Getting the seed underground will help you attract top talent, increase employee engagement and retention efforts, and ultimately create a strong organizational culture. The guiding principles to effectively doing this are:

- Empowerment.
- Career enhancement.
- Collaboration.

In the absence of an effective machine running smoothly, it's nearly impossible to excel at all three. You can't just suddenly empower people, enhance their careers, and create a culture of collaboration because it sounds like a great idea. It's a multipronged process that takes time to develop and implement. This type of organizational culture doesn't happen overnight, and the ingredients vary by industry. The processes and systems for each of these intangibles of development depend on the type of business, the culture you wish to create, the talent necessary to best serve your customer, the environment you work in (union, non-union), and a variety of other factors.

You might say, "I have an opening to fill. I need a person in there quick, and I don't have a lot of time to train them."

I like to say, "Don't step over a dollar to pick up a dime." If you are so focused on yielding the crop and not willing to get the seed in the ground, you will constantly be hiring and firing, and your busyness will only get worse.

In *Procrastinate on Purpose*, Rory Vaden teaches leaders the value of purposeful procrastination. Sometimes you have to put off something pressing to do something that will pay back residual returns. A great example of this is hiring, training, and developing your workforce. If you can get employees (and volunteers, if you're a nonprofit) to come to you, stick around, and flourish, you can reduce operating expenses, mitigate opportunity costs, and improve overall service.

Just as attracting, developing, and retaining top talent is financially beneficial to your organization, so is retaining customers. This principle of getting the seed in the ground doesn't apply only to your employees, it also applies to your customers.

Each customer has a customer lifetime value (CLV). Knowing what that is will give you a new perspective on customer retention. As an example, we'll say your company generates $3,000 each year per customer. Let's assume it costs $500 to acquire that customer and they have an average lifespan of ten years as your customer. Your company's CLV would be $3,000 x 10 - $500 = $29,500.

It costs an average of five times more to replace a customer than it does to retain a customer. Just as there are a number of ways to attract, develop, and retain your best talent, there are also retention strategies to retain customers and create routine response behavior, where the consumer makes an automatic purchase decision based on information they have gathered from the past. For example, if the consumer has a pizza app on their mobile device and wants pizza, they automatically purchase it based on routine response behavior. This can be said for church attendance, services, car buying, beverages, and so forth.

Ultimately you must structure the machine in a way that makes it easy to do business with you. Your customers do not need to see the parts, gears, and axles (the processes and systems) of the machine. They need a seamless, convenient, and easy buying experience with great value and service from your empowered and outstanding talent. Once the consumer has a great buying experience, you have the opportunity to create a buying habit. Companies that offer loyalty programs can shift customers' behavior and create routine response behaviors, ultimately retaining the customer and a solid CLV.

New customers and employees come into your organization and say, "Now what?" They are the seeds that have the potential to grow into thriving crops. But if your machine, processes, and systems are not set up to get that seed in the ground quickly, it will easily get blown away or picked off by the birds or—in the case of modern business—snatched up by the competition and recruiters for other companies.

What It Looks like with Real People

An excellent illustration of having an onboarding process or system is the member retention strategy we have created in the Christian Chamber. I accepted the offer to become president just before the COVID-19 pandemic shut down the world as we knew it in March 2020. That same month, my dad passed away. In June, I assumed my new position, leading a rapidly declining organization. If one were to look at the Chamber on a product life cycle scale, it was at the rate of decline nearing extinction.

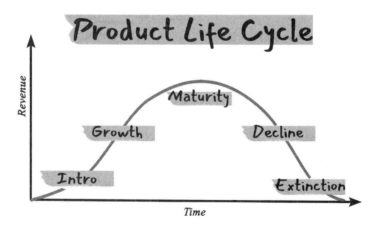

The money coming in was not enough to pay my salary. So, for months, I pulled money from my personal savings to support my daughter and myself while I worked tirelessly to turn the organization around.

I came from running an operation with a multimillion-dollar budget where we had functionalized departments for everything—corporate communications, accounting, legal, human resources, you name it—so experts were easily accessible. However, in the Chamber, it was just me, and I was keenly aware that I did not know enough and alone was not enough to make a difference. Still, I was passionate about the mission and hungry to make it succeed, so I jumped in with no clue about this type of industry. When feelings of *What have I done?* threatened to overwhelm me, I was softly reminded in my spirit, "Forget about what you want, focus on what you have, and allow God to provide you with what you need."

This word came from "Ridiculous Faith," a message series taught by Pastor Craig Groeschel in 2015. The premise of this teaching is found in 2 Kings 4. A newly widowed woman was on the brink of losing both of her sons into slavery to repay her late husband's debt. When Elisha asked her what she had, she said she had "nothing in the house except a jar of oil" (2 Kings 4:2, NASB). He then told her to gather empty jars. She obediently gathered jars, the oil began to flow, and she filled all the empty jars she had gathered with the oil that was flowing out. When the empty jars were all full, the oil stopped.

I wonder if she would have gathered more empty jars if she had known there were an endless supply of oil for each empty jar. Pastor Don Cousins said, "Faith moves the hand of God." When you continue to focus on God and not what you lack, God provides you with precisely what you need. The moral of the story is that we should stay focused on the resources and assets that we have and demonstrate faith in God by completely surrendering our expectations and resources to Him. I have heard it said this way: God can do more with 90 percent than I can with 100 percent.

The message was so powerful that I remember writing it down and saying it over and over. The seed that was planted in 2015 came to harvest six years later.

I had members who loved the Christian Chamber as much as I did and wanted to see it succeed. They came out of the woodwork asking to help. With volunteers and members, I started creating systems and programs to plug people into areas they were passionate about. In the middle of a global pandemic, we started growing.

Next, I recruited a high-functioning board that gave me access to business gurus in their respective industries. Now I had insight into the functional areas I had been missing.

As we recruited new members, we created a member onboarding system that included a handwritten letter, an email, introduction in our newsletter so existing members could welcome them, and an invitation to Kingdom Commerce University (KCU) so each new member or customer could quickly move from lying on the ground (like the seed on the path) to being covered under rich soil (an environment for retention and engagement).

They didn't need to see the processes or systems we were creating, they needed the answer to, "What now?" For example, at her first Chamber event, Madelyn Weed from Catholic Charities said, "As soon as I signed up, I got an email from the president, I got a letter in the mail, I got an invitation to KCU, and I got a call from a member. I'm an introvert, and when I walked into this meeting today, I felt like I was walking in among friends." That was a clear demonstration of how well our onboarding system works.

The guidance I found in the Parable of the Sower helped me turn this organization around to where we are now as a national organization helping strengthen and support other Christian chambers and, in turn, Christian business leaders around the US. It didn't happen overnight, and it wasn't easy. But we needed to plant our new members in rich soil that would allow them to take firm root in our organization and grow.

||||||||||||||||||||||||||||||||||||||||||||||||||||||||||||||||||||||||||||||||||||||||||||||||||||||

THE COST TO RETAIN AN EMPLOYEE, VOLUNTEER, BOARD MEMBER, OR CUSTOMER IS MUCH LESS THAN THE COST TO REPLACE THEM.

||||||||||||||||||||||||||||||||||||||||||||||||||||||||||||||||||||||||||||||||||||||||||||||||||||||

The cost to retain an employee, volunteer, board member, or customer is much less than the cost to replace them. That's why a strategic onboarding process for employees, customers, and volunteers is critical in engagement. Make this part of the machine. You can't afford to leave it to chance.

CHAPTER 4

COMMUNICATION
IS THE WATER
FOR YOUR SEEDS

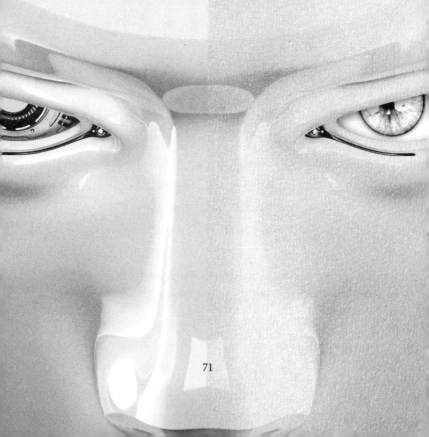

THE

BEST

ROBOT

WINS

s important as it is to plant your seeds (people) in rich soil so they can grow, your work doesn't stop there. The soil is only the first step.

> *A farmer went out to sow his seed. As he was scattering the seed, some fell along the path; it was trampled on, and the birds ate it up. Some fell on rocky ground, and when it came up, the plants withered because they had no moisture. Other seed fell among thorns, which grew up with it and choked the plants. Still other seed fell on good soil. It came up and yielded a crop, a hundred times more than was sown. —Luke 8:5-8 (NIV)*

Some of the seed fell on rocky ground, and when it came up, the plants withered because they had no moisture.

A seed planted in rich soil will sprout, but if it isn't watered regularly, it will wilt and won't produce a crop. In your organization, communication is the water for your crop, and the entire crop needs it.

Communication Source

Frontline Worker

As you can see in the image of a watering system, the plants closest to the water source are receiving the most moisture, making them grow and flourish. The plants down the irrigation row farthest away from the water source are not receiving any water and are not getting the moisture they need.

Now imagine this is your organizational hierarchy. The plants farthest from the water source represent the employees farthest from the CEO. Communication in an organization is the water source for your human capital. When you think about the machine's gears, you could even consider communication the oil which produces the lubrication for the gears, axles, and parts. Or in the case of a business, the oil between the systems, processes, and people. Communication will keep all these things flowing smoothly. It's vital for your organization and humans to flourish.

Creating a collaborative culture is done in part by the willingness of a leader to value and seek communication from the frontline workers. However, effective communication isn't just top-down. You must create a culture of communication that is fluid within the organization. Picture a recirculation pump.

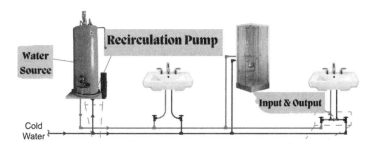

When I moved to Florida, it was December. My house did not have the natural gas I was used to, but rather a propane tank. When I walked across the wood floor in my bare feet, I could feel areas under the floor that were warm. In doing my research to figure out why, I learned that there was a recirculation pump circulating water from two hot water tanks throughout the house in a process that keeps the water constantly warm. The idea is that every faucet produces instant hot water—there's no waiting for the water to warm up. It's a great concept but instant hot water takes a lot of energy to create. One day I needed hot water, but there wasn't any.

I had drained the propane tank in a matter of weeks after moving into my new house.

My point in sharing this is that it takes effort and energy to have fluid communication in your organization. There is value in information coming up from the customer touchpoints to the individuals making the policy, training, and investment decisions in your organization. As soon as the customer turns the spigot, the water should be warm, meaning your organization needs to empower your employees to address and adapt to your consumers' needs. That should then feed back up to the top levels of the organization to ensure consistency across the organization, creating an enterprise state of mind and a culture of communication and collaboration.

HUMAN WORKERS ARE ON THE FRONTLINE OF YOUR ORGANIZATION.

Human workers are on the frontline of your organization. They are customer-facing; they are the eyes, ears, and touchpoints of your company. If they don't have the tools to succeed, they will not execute the organization's mission the intended way. If they don't feel there is a place to be heard, you will not have a full grasp of what your customers are experiencing. You don't want to miss the opportunity to communicate with them and to hear from them. Because people determine the potential in an organization, rich and flowing communication will strengthen your human workers by giving them the confidence and tools needed to execute the mission and by giving the leaders assurance the systems and processes are working correctly.

Just like the seed not reaching a harvest when it fell among the cracks, if communication is only flowing down and not engaging the entire workforce, you will isolate and lose employees. Your customer-facing human workers have touchpoints and get feedback directly from the consumer. If the machine does not foster a working environment where communication is ever-present and flowing, the people creating the processes and systems—the decision-makers, innovators, and change-makers—will never know there is an opportunity or problem within the machine.

When I consult with a company and gather intel, I spend time with the frontline workers. It's not uncommon for them to share information about challenges they are experiencing in trying to best serve the customers. Frontline workers know more about what the customer is experiencing with a company; however, they usually don't have the power or authority to create policies, implement training, or allocate funds.

Some companies pay for mining software to listen to calls for keywords or common issues, then use that to generate training or gather information. This provides a lagging systematic approach to getting intel about the customers' experiences, but that alone is only as good as your ability to mine for the correct data, evaluate trends, and react to the data. It doesn't empower people and create a culture of collaboration and communication.

The lagging indicators of employee and customer surveys are additional tools used to gather data. While it's important to have this information, what you get will only be as good as the questions you ask. When done right, surveys can be a helpful tool, but if they're not worded correctly or acted on quickly, they can be harmful to the workforce and create a relational breakdown between management and employees.

A perfect example of creating a culture of collaboration and communication came about as a little bit of an accident. When I started my job as vice president of the West Texas region, I was well-versed on customer service, but I didn't have any experience in the field operations of running a natural gas distribution company.

Remember the manager I reported to when I was a secretary? While he didn't believe I could transition to the field, God made a way for that to happen—years later and on a much bigger scale than either of us could conceive at the time. "The Lord does not look at the things people look at. People look at the outward appearance, but the Lord looks at the heart" (1 Samuel 16:7, NIV).

God doesn't call the qualified; He qualifies the called. I had a series of interviews for the job and an entire day at the corporate office with C-suite executives. One, who later became a great friend and advocate, said, "How on earth do you think you are going to lead field employees when you don't even know what they do?"

I kept the interview focused on leadership and leading people. One of the questions I was asked was, "How do you define success?"

I said, "It's not about what I am going to do. I define success by what I leave behind."

He later told me that answer sealed the deal for his vote for me.

My final interview of that grueling day was with the CEO of this multibillion dollar company. When I saw his name on my interview schedule, my stomach flipped over.

I'll never forget that interview. The conference room had floor-to-ceiling windows overlooking downtown Tulsa. The conference table was the biggest I'd ever seen—and I still haven't seen one bigger. The CEO strode in confidently, wearing a white button-up shirt and pressed trousers. He was bigger in person than he appeared in pictures. Though he was smiling, I could tell he was reading me from the minute he walked in the door. I was wearing my best navy suit, pantyhose, pearls, and heels. Naturally, I was nervous, but I tried to mirror his confidence with my smile and a firm handshake.

We had thirty minutes scheduled. He asked me one question.

I knew if I didn't stay in that room for the entire time, I was sunk. The question he asked was, "What questions do you have for me?"

This was a dream come true for me. I had a ton of questions prepared and strategically talked about myself in our verbal tennis match.

The president called me the next day. He asked, "How do you think the interviews went?" When I replied that I thought they went well, he continued, "They must have because *they* want to offer you the job." It was clear he did not include himself in the "they" that were offering me the job. I didn't know if I should have been excited or offended. I chose excited.

I was nervous about moving to El Paso in 2009. It was right at the height of the war with the cartels in Juarez, Mexico, a stone's throw away from El Paso. On my first day on the job, I was greeted with curious looks and smiles. My new office had windows looking out to the Franklin Mountains, but my view was interrupted by what appeared to be bullet holes in the glass. There was another one on my computer monitor. That's when I laughed. One of my new directors was quite a prankster (the bullet holes were fake), and immediately I felt at home.

As I began my role as vice president, I was not an expert or even experienced in the jobs I was responsible for. I inherited an existing group of direct reports and didn't have the opportunity to build my team. So even though I understood people, the budget, the headcount, and the metrics, there was so much more to learn. The president, my boss at the time, told me I needed to get out and learn the business. So, I got my hard hat and personal protective equipment (PPE) and started riding along with all the departments.

The first department I went with was meter reading. We started our day a little after 5:30 a.m. Jose, the meter reader I was with, wore a huge smile and carried a little backpack stocked with a small radio, binoculars, and a couple of waters for us. Since the meter readers walked the routes that didn't have automated meter reading technology, it made more financial sense to load a group of meter readers in a single vehicle and drop them off in their respective routes. We were dropped off in a highly populated mountainous area in the city of El Paso and hit the ground walking.

We read more than 650 meters that day. We greeted people, dodged scary dogs, and saw interesting things like an empty piece of armor. As we walked, we talked, and I got to know Jose. He told me stories about his life, his why for getting up every day and working in the job, and his talents, gifts, and dreams. He was highly intelligent, hardworking—a huge asset to the organization. He was loyal, dedicated, and had some innovative ideas for improving the meter-reading process with automation, increased safety, and more.

Those thousands of steps with Jose let me walk away with valuable knowledge about an important area of the business. Yes, I was tired, but more than anything, I was hungry to learn about another department and the people who made the business function. Next was service, then construction, pressure control and maintenance, engineering, and collections.

Each time I was out with the employees, in addition to learning about their jobs, I was learning about them and their families, hearing stories of the organization, and gaining an essential perspective just as I did when I was a new supervisor in the call center, but on a different scale. As I was spending time with the frontline workers, I kept hearing a common theme over and over: "I wish my supervisor would come out and do this with me."

I gathered up my director team and asked: "How often are we in the field with our employees?"

The answer was as I expected: "We're too busy with paperwork."

Remember we talked about task versus people orientation. One is not better than the other, but there must be balance. Typically, engineers lean toward task, for which we should all be thankful. We want the people constructing bridges and pipelines to pay attention to details, processes, systems, and numbers. Leaders that have a strong disposition toward task will naturally spend more time with paperwork than with people. At the time, the company's leaders were more focused on the systems and processes than on the human workers. That left the workers without the "moisture" the seed needs to grow.

The organization had become focused on process and systems because that's where the leadership team was most comfortable and therefore spent most (if not all) of its time. With a lot of persuasion, I was able to get the director team to buy into a new program we rolled out in the West Texas region called the Ride-Along Program. Because I was working around so many task-oriented leaders, I couldn't leave the very important human connection to chance, so we formalized the program to ensure we could give leaders a clinical approach to connecting with the human workers.

Each director, supervisor, and manager in the organization committed to ninety-six hours of ride-along cross functionally, meaning the supervisor of a team that turns on new service for customers might be out with employees that read meters or sitting in the call center with customer service agents speaking directly to the customers. This was not a gotcha program; it was enrichment, teaching task-oriented leaders to connect with people and giving people (the seeds) the water they needed to flourish.

Each month, we connected in person and online to discuss our experiences in the field. We rewarded the first leader that hit the ninety-six hours (he was a people-oriented leader). We charted each employee in the organization to ensure each of the 380 employees had an opportunity to have a ride-along, resulting in thousands of hours poured into our employees and workgroup.

Once the employees realized that we were doing this to improve, not to catch them doing something wrong, they were excited to have that one-on-one time to be heard and be known. So, it wasn't uncommon for me to be out and have an employee stop me and say, "I haven't had my ride-along yet."

I was presenting a quarterly update in a meeting with about eighty field employees present. One of the construction guys raised his hand to ask a question. I don't recall the question, but I remember that he followed it with, "I bet you don't even know my name."

I said, "Well, Roy, let me answer that for you."

Everyone in the room snickered when I said his name.

Knowing the names of the people who work for you may seem like a minor thing when you're running a multimillion dollar utility, but it's not. People love to hear their names. When the senior people make the effort to learn names and faces, it enhances overall communication as it creates loyalty and a sense of belonging among the workers. The president, my boss at the time, understood the value of knowing and saying a person's name. He was an engineer by trade, so he approached learning names systematically and clinically. On my first day as vice president, he made sure I got a notebook filled with color pictures and names of 380 employees. While the intention and process worked for him, my technique was more face-to-face, talking with people, hearing stories and nicknames, learning about the individuals working on the team, and remembering their names because I knew them as individuals.

Roy always stood out. He was the informal leader of the group and more vocal than most. Informal leaders have a great power to persuade and lead the team—often more than those with the title and official authority—and I respected Roy's leadership ability and commitment to the company. Even though he didn't realize it, as I was getting to know him and others by listening to stories shared within the organization, I made it a point to learn Roy's and many others' names. That I had done so was a big deal to him and his team.

The Ride-Along Program revealed opportunities to implement several best practices and new safety initiatives that we rolled out all over the West Texas region. It gave employees a sense of belonging, it increased employee engagement, and it opened the door for innovative ideas, new systems, enhanced safety initiatives, and processes to help our employees succeed, improve working conditions, break down functional silos, enhance communication, and better serve our customers.

The Ride-Along Program was such a huge success that it was featured in the *ONEOK Quarterly* magazine.

GETTING TO KNOW YOU

TEXAS GAS SERVICE'S 'RIDE-ALONG' PROGRAM BRINGS EMPLOYEES AND SUPERVISORS CLOSER TOGETHER

Texas Gas Service employees have taken Becoming ONE and **The Journey** to a new level. They are getting to know each other as

Above: Krystal Parker had the idea for the Texas Gas Service Ride-Along program when she became regional vice president and wanted to gain operational knowledge.

Source: ONEOK Quarterly Fall 2012 page 9-10

When we started making plans and setting goals for the following year, the support for doing the program again was unanimous.

Our goal was to have 5 percent of the leaders' time spent in cross-functional training, development, and collaboration during the program. One of the greatest outcomes of this program and why it was so successful was that the communication in the organization started looking like the recirculation pump moving conversation and collaboration around the company, department to department, person to person, creating an enterprise state of mind and providing the water our seeds needed to grow.

Make It Safe to Communicate

An organization's problems and failures provide the most incredible opportunities for innovation. Unfortunately, it's not uncommon for issues to be driven underground and not reported or resolved simply because the leader did not foster a communication culture, and people didn't feel safe asking questions and making suggestions.

The company's senior-level meetings typically consisted of about fifty-eight men in suits and a handful of women. When I became a vice president and was required to attend those meetings, another officer who had been with the company a long time offered me this advice: "Whatever you do, do *not* draw attention to yourself.

The CEO might ask if there are questions, but do not ask anything, don't even make eye contact."

At my first meeting, I followed the instructions. At the second meeting, I decided to see what would happen if I raised my hand and asked a question when the CEO opened the floor. I had a legitimate question about the issues being discussed, so I put my hand in the air when he asked for questions. He did a double take when he saw my hand go up. I think he was intrigued and maybe even amused that the new, young vice president was speaking up, and he responded with a respectful, appropriate answer. So, at the next meeting, I asked another question.

I wasn't necessarily trying to be noticed, but I didn't want to just blend in. I genuinely wanted to understand certain things. I knew the better equipped I was as a corporate officer, the more I could advocate for and lead my team in West Texas. While I never experienced the wrath of the CEO for asking a question, the stories told in the organization would have had me believe different if I hadn't tested it for myself. I was being onboarded through stories and the culture as an officer. If I were not a risk-taker, I may have never spoken up and instead simply blended in with everyone else.

While my intentions were to garner support and awareness for West Texas, I became the direct beneficiary of that courage to speak up. As time went on, I was selected to attend Harvard Business

School to get a certification in leadership for senior executives. Remember, God doesn't call the qualified; He qualifies the called.

Regardless of who you are as a leader, there is a narrative about you flowing through the walls of your organization. If employees are not risk-takers like I am, you may never hear the truth in the organization.

‖‖

TRAIN AND ENABLE YOUR TEAM TO BE PROBLEM-SEE-ERS AND PROBLEM-SOLVERS.

‖‖

Train and enable your team to be problem-see-ers and problem-solvers. How you see problems and failures will determine your ability to experience innovation, so as the leader, you want to know what's wrong. How you see God will determine your ability to experience supernatural innovation—meaning your conversations with God cannot just be one way, either. You need communication flowing with God daily, just like the recirculation pump. God abiding in you and your business will supernaturally position you for success with new insights and ideas. It's vital for you as a leader to foster a workplace environment that celebrates communication, problems, and failures.

I have worked with leaders who work all month on a presentation or a big email for employees and have very little communication aside from that one event. They wonder why employees didn't do what they were told to do after the meeting was over or the email sent out.

Your employees want and need you to reach them where and how they are most susceptible to receiving information and communication. Simply put, there is no one silver-bullet approach to communicating with your human workers. Connect with your employees through email, text, virtual team meetings, virtual one-on-one sessions, video, conference calls, direct messages, and more. Do not rely on just one medium or touchpoint to communicate with your employees but use multiple sources with multiple styles.

There are many communication barriers, and they multiply when you add in the virtual element of distractions and personal filters. Dr. Albert Mehrabian deduced that communication is only 7 percent *what* you say, and the remainder is *how* you say it. If body language and tone make up 93 percent of the conversation and you are only communicating on email or through conference calls where you talk or type *at* your employees, you are likely not being heard. One of my mentors, Kari French, used to say, "Over-communicate to make up for the complexity of structure."

If you think you are communicating adequately today with everything that's competing for a person's attention, you need to amplify your communication efforts by ten. Remember, the fortune is in the follow-up. After a meeting, follow up with a brief and concise email, auto call, or video detailing expectations and project assignments. It's also important to note that there is no disaggregation in communication for your employees or customers. You need to meet them where they are and where they wish to communicate with you. Multiple mediums for communication should be used to reach your employees and customers.

When you succeed at communication, you will likely see more problems than before. You should celebrate this because it's where the opportunities to innovate exist. An organization with fluid communication across all levels can adapt and innovate more quickly than an organization that buries issues and failures. Whether you choose to deal with them or not, they still exist. It's okay to disagree.

||||||||||||||||||||||||||||||||||||||||||||||||||||||||||||||||||||||||||||||||||||||||||||||||||||||||||||||

AN ORGANIZATION WITH FLUID COMMUNICATION ACROSS ALL LEVELS CAN ADAPT AND INNOVATE MORE QUICKLY THAN AN ORGANIZATION THAT BURIES ISSUES AND FAILURES.

||||||||||||||||||||||||||||||||||||||||||||||||||||||||||||||||||||||||||||||||||||||||||||||||||||||||||||||

One final note on communication: encourage constructive abrasion.

When people think of communication, they often envision harmonious conversations where everyone holds hands and sings kumbaya. However, leaders who encourage constructive or creative abrasion as a form of communication can foster an environment of collaborative communication and are more likely to anticipate and leverage issues, opportunities, and threats in the organization.

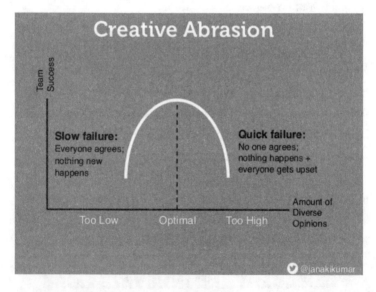

Retrieved from https://www.slideshare.net/UXSTRAT/ux-strat-usa-janaki-kumar-creating-a-culture-of-designled-innovation

When I went to Harvard Business School for Senior Executives, the course focused on innovation, globalization, and leadership diversity. The classroom was filled with more than sixty people from twenty-one different countries. The majority of the students were business owners and C-suite-level employees. Every day we sat at a U-shaped table, and the instructors encouraged us to have creative abrasion. This was the first time I'd heard the term, and I remember thinking to myself, "Isn't abrasion bad?" When I tried to stir up some creative abrasion at my staunch bureaucratic company, it wasn't uncommon for people to get offended by me delighting in the challenging conversations and brainstorming sessions.

I cannot stress to you enough: creative abrasion is a must for innovation. When creative abrasion is not present, it often signifies a fear culture where employees don't feel empowered to speak up. That can kill a company. Steve Jobs, while tough, was one of the most inspiring and challenging leaders. If Jobs went along to get along, do you think we would all enjoy carrying around our iPhones today?

When Netflix CEO Reed Hastings raised prices to separate DVD and digital streaming, he lost over eight hundred thousand subscribers. That may have been a bit much abrasion, but his vision and bravery helped us all quit paying late fees and put Blockbuster out of business.

A perfect example of this happening in my career was when I was involved in a complete reorganization where nearly three thousand employees were impacted with a title change, supervisor change, location change, and more. We took this very change-resistant organization from a geographic-based organizational structure to a function-based structure.

For example, I was the vice president of operations for West Texas and customer service for all of Texas. I was responsible for engineering, operations, outside service, corrosion, pressure control and maintenance, construction, meter reading, billing, collections, business development, customer service call center, rates and regulatory, community relations, and the list goes on. When we redesigned the organization to function, I was handed all customer service, billing, web, and collections (union and non-union) for three states with very different setups. My task was to create the organizational chart (titles, pay, reporting locations, supervisor structure, etc.). Another vice president was given all operations, another all engineering, and so forth. The biggest opportunity in making this change was to become experts in our field. The greatest risk was silos.

On my first day in the redesigned organization, my boss told me to close all the customer service centers in two states and leave only one open.

I had worked with the customer service teams in Kansas and Texas, and those were the two states I was directed to close. The area I was to reconstruct customer service at was in Oklahoma and, for the most part, it was unknown to me. But from my experience in the other two states, I was intimately familiar with the company's strengths and weaknesses; I knew the pockets of genius and the areas of risk. To sum it up, I knew the organizational DNA, so I quickly got up to speed on Oklahoma. I used that knowledge to counter my job assignment with a new and very outside-the-box response. In 2013, I was able to show my boss that the future of customer service was not bound by bricks and mortar. Instead of arguing against the closures and consolidating into one state, I proposed a multifaceted seven-step transformation initiative connecting agents in the cloud.

Not only did it save jobs, but my proposal also saved the company over $1 million in operating expenses and improved and enhanced customer service offerings.

I firmly believe if I had just followed orders and not leaned into constructive and creative abrasion for communication, I would have been fired. Closing centers and moving to one building would have crushed our JD Power Award-winning customer service, cost millions of dollars, angered regulators, unhinged union relations in other parts of the company, created a mass exodus of employees, and more. My ability to offer an entrepreneurial transformation initiative was due in part to my keen understanding and awareness of each organization's resources, capabilities, and culture. I effectively grabbed the pockets of genius from all three states, expanded on the good, put out the risks, and connected the team in the cloud to create one voice and a seamless and enjoyable experience for the customer.

To assess the communication culture in your organization, ask these questions:

- Is communication top-down with primarily one medium used, or is it flowing throughout the organization with media richness?
- Is there a way to communicate problems and issues from all levels in the organization?
- Do people at all levels feel their ideas are welcomed and appreciated?
- Do you have multiple vehicles in place for suggestions?
- Do employees feel that they can safely communicate on any topic without retaliation?
- Is disagreement unwelcome and seen as a form of conflict creation?
- Is creative abrasion encourage?

I don't need to tell you what your answers should be. Let these questions be a starting point for analyzing and improving communication throughout your organization. After all, you don't know who on your team has a better idea than you unless you foster a culture of collaborative communication that celebrates creative and innovative ideas. Encourage creative abrasion. It ain't personal, it's just good business.

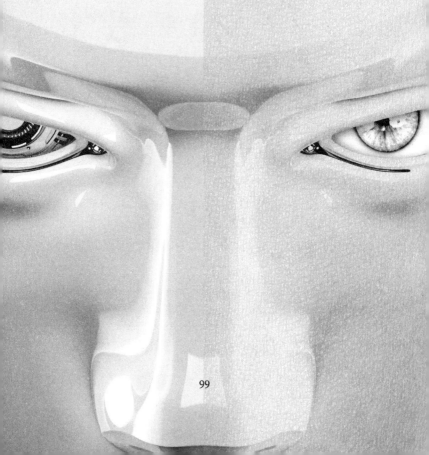

CHAPTER 5

DON'T CHOKE YOUR SEEDS

THE

BEST

ROBOT

WINS

Y ou can hire great people and communicate effectively, yet your systems can stifle creativity, innovation, and productivity.

A farmer went out to sow his seed. As he was scattering the seed, some fell along the path; it was trampled on, and the birds ate it up. Some fell on rocky ground, and when it came up, the plants withered because they had no moisture. Other seed fell among thorns, which grew up with it and choked the plants. Still other seed fell on good soil. It came up and yielded a crop, a hundred times more than was sown." —Luke 8:5-8 (NIV)

The thorns in this parable represent the processes and systems in your organization. Processes and systems are essential for an organization to succeed, but a strength out of control can become a weakness, and too much of a good thing can be a bad thing.

If you're not careful, processes and systems can choke the seed— your human workers. Without awareness, leaders frequently create more policies, rules, and processes to control work, measure output, mitigate risk, and fix a one-off problem than are necessary. It's common for organizations to add processes and never remove them. Humans follow the rules and don't ask why. They spend year after year doing a process and not understanding how it aligns with the overall goals or outcomes of the organization—and sometimes it doesn't.

I love to ask the question, "Why do you do this?"

The answer I usually get is, "That's how we've always done it." That's not a good reason.

Out-of-control systems and processes slow down the machine. The time and effort it takes to get an answer, make a decision, or even create an invoice can crush creativity and the innovative spirit of the humans in your organization. This, in turn, negatively impacts the service you give your customers.

Innovation Lies in Simplicity

Set expectations and rely on your measurements—but keep it simple. Innovation lies in simplicity.

Complexity crushes innovation. Processes can quickly become more complex. You have to be intentional about keeping things simple to foster an environment where your seed can flourish.

You also need to be able to set expectations and measure performance effectively. Leaders can fall into wanting to micromanage employees in the absence of measurements, creating a company bogged down with too much bureaucracy and unnecessary controls.

Companies do not drift into simplicity. It's not uncommon for a policy to be created because someone made a poor decision. Then another mistake is made, another policy is created, and before long, something simple is overcomplicated and arduous.

COMPLEXITY AND MISGUIDED STRUCTURE CAN MAKE A SIMPLE TASK LABORIOUS AND DIFFICULT.

This is something we've been struggling with for centuries. Moses came down from the mountain with only ten commandments. But over time, those ten simple commandments evolved into hundreds, if not thousands, of laws. By creating erroneous rules and laws, the people had turned something intended for good into something completely different—something Jesus explained quite clearly in the temple when He demonstrated righteous anger by flipping tables and yelling. Complexity and misguided structure can make a simple task laborious and difficult.

Before the first bicycle, there was a unicycle. For it to go faster, the one wheel grew until they came up with bike chains and added a second wheel for speed and performance. The longer the bike chain, the more seats are needed to create the inertia to propel the bike forward. Imagine if, in your organization, each one of those chain links represents a policy and rule. The more policies and rules you have, the slower the process becomes.

Microsoft was a bloated, process-heavy, bureaucratic organization when Satya Nadella took over. In a town hall, he told employees that they should skip meetings they'd been invited to if they didn't need to be there. He also advised workers to bring things to him directly if they felt stifled by the bureaucracy. Microsoft had become top-heavy and slow-moving, and it was choking the seed nearly to extinction.

When Nadella came on board, he wrote this in a letter to employees:

> *Our industry does not respect tradition—it only respects innovation. This is a critical time for the industry and for Microsoft. Make no mistake, we are headed for greater places—as technology evolves and we evolve with and ahead of it.*

Nadella instituted one of the largest layoffs in Microsoft's history, letting eighteen thousand employees go. He said that Microsoft would "have fewer layers of management, both top-down and side-ways, to accelerate the flow of information and decision-making." He understood that thorns could choke out creativity, innovation, and speed. Nadella was named Microsoft CEO in 2014. Today, he is known for leading the company through a complete corporate turnaround and making it one of the most valuable companies in the world (at least for now).

Much of Nadella's success can be attributed to his understanding that processes and systems were needed to support employees, not slow them down. Nadella understood that processes and systems should be used to help employees focus on purpose and mission over rules and compliance.

If you understand the mission and vision for the organization and keep that top of mind, you'll be able to structure processes and systems to best accomplish the goal. Often, leaders become so focused on the processes and systems to control costs and employees that they lose sight of the mission and impede the ability to execute the mission. Breathing is to life like profits are to a business; while breathing is not the purpose of living, it is essential for life. Just as profits are not the purpose for which the business exists, they are essential for the organization to survive. Ultimately you have to remember why your organization exists and structure your processes and systems in a way to help your people accomplish that task. It's healthy to make a profit but not at the expense of destroying your ability to accomplish the mission. Profit cannot have a higher position over purpose. I see leaders with so many measures and policies in place they suffocate the creativity and innovation right out of their human capital.

Measuring performance is critical, but not for the reasons you may think. Misguided leaders think measurement is to control employees or monitor human capital as they would the stock market. Effective measurement will support the employees, provide purpose for their jobs by reinforcing alignment to the mission, help measure organizational slack, and free up the leader to work on complex problems to stay ahead of the competition. Helping your human workers know the goals and expectations and providing the tools for them to be successful will help them feel empowered with the freedom to succeed. Employee engagement and retention are byproducts of successful measurements that spark intrinsic motivation among your employees. Having the proper measurements in place will free up the leader to inspect what they expect, move the dial on performance and, most importantly, recognize, reward, and celebrate successful outcomes.

As a leader, you should identify when targets are out of reach and quickly redirect and coach when a teammate is not progressing toward the goal. Simplicity helps keep the company agile and the machine operating at peak performance.

Innovation lies in your people, your problems, and simplicity. You may have heard of Palo Alto Research Center (PARC). In the 1970s, Xerox created PARC and staffed it with the most incredible minds to innovate new products. The research center became widely known and caught the attention of Steve Jobs. Upon a visit to PARC in 1979, Jobs was introduced to the personal computer, mouse, and graphical user interface (GUI). Immediately, he knew Xerox was sitting on a gold mine.

In 1983, Apple introduced the Lisa commercial computer, equipped with a GUI and a mouse. Are you wondering why, if Xerox invented the first PC, they are not dominating the personal computer space? As Jobs said, "Xerox was run by toner heads who had no real idea of what they were looking at. Had they real-ized this, Xerox could have owned the entire personal computer industry today."

The engineers knew they had created something special but cutting through the bureaucracy and cumbersome processes to garner support from the top brass for this product was almost impossible in the Xerox organization. They had the foresight to see the value of creating this team to address innovation, but then they created bureaucracy, i.e., thorns and thistles, that choked out the idea from ever seeing the light of day. By contrast, Apple was nimble and able to adapt quickly. As a result, Apple was able to dominate in that space.

The key to unlocking creativity and innovation is to build trust. Trust is built through a variety of communication methods and clearly set expectations. Trust is *not* built by creating a complex and cumbersome organization that chokes out creativity in your human workers.

Getting to Simple

As important as your systems and processes are for your success, your customers don't care about them. They care about getting quality products and services delivered in an honest, ethical manner. It's your job as a leader to create systems and processes to improve a customer's experience and get maximum engagement from your human workers. Simplicity is one true way to ensure your systems and processes can support the people. You can simplify your business in six ways.

1) Be sure every process and rule you have in place, every decision you make, aligns with your company's purpose and mission.

   Why do you do the things you do? If something doesn't align with your company's purpose and mission, either stop it or change it. This means asking tough and sometimes painful questions, but it must be done.

2) Make it easy to do business with you.

Simplify the processes for your customers to deal with you and simplify the internal processes that are in place to serve your customers. For example, make it easy for customers to contact you and empower your people to do what's necessary to respond to them.

3) Eliminate redundancy.

Look for places where multiple people are doing the same function and consolidate and streamline if you can. Of course, you need backups and cross-training, but cut out superfluous functions.

4) Eliminate unnecessary meetings and bureaucracy.

Be sure every meeting is necessary and give people permission not to go to a meeting when their presence is not productive. If you don't know the reason for a process, figure it out—and if it's not required, stop doing it.

5) Look at every position, understand the greater need, ask tough questions, and keep positions fluid.

Often, we get comfortable with positions in a company and don't even think to ask if there is a way to add technology and utilize this person or position for another more important role that aligns with the company's mission. As your mission, technology, and customers' needs evolve, so will your staff's roles, job descriptions, and expectations of their performance.

6) Assess how you as the leader are spending your time.
Be sure that your time is spent working *on* the business, not *in* the business. Leaders should spend their time doing things that are strategic, innovative, mission-driven, creating value for your customers and employees, solving complex problems and creating a culture rich in communication and collaboration spanning across the enterprise.

Think about the Ten Commandments. When Jesus was asked which was the most important commandment, He said:

> *"Love the Lord your God with all your heart and with all your soul and with all your mind." This is the first and greatest commandment. And the second is like it: "Love your neighbor as yourself." All the Law and the Prophets hang on these two commandments. —Matthew 22:37–39 (NIV)*

It really is that simple—in life and in business. But no organization, no business, naturally drifts toward simplicity as it grows. It will get more complex. What we must do as leaders is examine what we're doing in the organization, understand the why, and simplify everywhere we can. Simplification and positional alignment with the organizational goals will make it easier for the leader to recognize the talent needed for a particular position. Simplification will also allow the individuals working in each position the satisfaction of knowing they can align their efforts to support the mission, giving them more job satisfaction.

Have you ever dialed into a call center with a problem you couldn't solve online? And then when you finally reach a human, they tell you they have to transfer you to someone else? It's maddening! But people don't go to work every day excited about how they'll get to frustrate customers—people want to do a good job, but sometimes they're working in a system that won't let them.

When you optimize the system, you improve service for your customers and help your human workers succeed. An example of this is how we optimized routes at the gas company. When we had a truck roll out of our yard, we knew the cost per mile, including the loaded labor cost of the employee driving the truck. We knew the best way to ensure our drivers were reducing safety incidents, improving timeliness to attend to customer needs, and reducing unnecessary miles driven, which kept the employee engaged and productive. By optimizing the system, we improved service to the customers; increased employee satisfaction, efficiency and engagement; reduced service costs; and remained competitive.

||||||||||||||||||||||||||||||||||||||||||||||||||||||||||||||||||||||||||||||||||||||||||||||||||||||||||||||

WHEN YOU OPTIMIZE THE SYSTEM, YOU IMPROVE SERVICE FOR YOUR CUSTOMERS AND HELP YOUR HUMAN WORKERS SUCCEED.

||||||||||||||||||||||||||||||||||||||||||||||||||||||||||||||||||||||||||||||||||||||||||||||||||||||||||||||

Customers want to turn on the faucet and have clean, affordable water pour out of the spigot. They don't care about the pipes, employees, rate cases, meters, service departments, and everything else it takes to make that happen. Systems and processes are necessary to create a business machine that runs smoothly. Customers don't need or want to see the intricate details behind creating a great product, service, or experience. *It ain't personal, it's just business.*

While systems and processes are vital to stabilize the organization and support your human workers, your customers don't care to see behind the curtain. For example, I live in Orlando. When we first moved here from Texas, we got season passes for Disney World, Universal, and SeaWorld. When visiting Universal's Harry Potter and the Forbidden Journey at Islands of Adventure, one of our favorites, my daughter and I got on the ride like we'd done countless times before. It sweeps you off your feet into a dazzling dark room filled with sounds and sights of mystical creatures as you experience flight with Harry and friends. It was going as planned until the ride suddenly stopped and we were tilted backwards in a way that left us looking up at one of the scary larger-than-life spiders. Fog filled the dark room and mysterious sounds filled my ears. I grabbed my daughter's hand because I knew that if I was feeling scared, she would be, too. As we held hands and waited, we went from a little scared to annoyed. Even though it was still pitch black, the music stopped, and we could hear voices. Workers were attempting to fix whatever had malfunctioned.

We lay facing upward with our legs dangling over the side of our pod, holding hands in the dark, hoping the ride would resume. But it didn't. Suddenly, the lights flipped on and the mystical environment disappeared, reduced to screens, pods with other passengers, strings, cables, concrete, projectors, and more. Once the method behind the magic was revealed, I couldn't close my eyes fast enough. I didn't want to know this. I wanted the mystery and the Forbidden Journey back.

As we moved through the rest of the ride with the lights on, I couldn't help but get my camera out and video a little, but I never posted it because I didn't want to ruin anyone else's experience.

When we finally got off the ride, a Universal rep handed everyone a cut-the-line pass to come back and experience the ride again that day. We were able to recapture the magic after the repairs were made.

This example is a perfect illustration of why systems and processes are vital to ensuring your customers receive seamless, effortless service with a smile. You cannot provide that if parts of the machine are not working properly. With so many moving parts in the machine, a leader needs to ensure they are working together at all times.

CHAPTER 6

WHEN YOU CREATE GOOD SOIL

THE

BEST

ROBOT

WINS

R emember, the soil represents your systems and processes, and the seed represents your human workers.

A farmer went out to sow his seed. As he was scattering the seed, some fell along the path; it was trampled on, and the birds ate it up. Some fell on rocky ground, and when it came up, the plants withered because they had no moisture. Other seed fell among thorns, which grew up with it and choked the plants. Still other seed fell on good soil. It came up and yielded a crop, a hundred times more than was sown. —Luke 8:5-8 (NIV)

When you create systems and processes that help your people be successful, you create the ability to yield a hundred times more than what was sown. By establishing the right structure and environment (building the right machine) to support the human elements in your business, you can operate at peak performance. It's vital that you get the seed (the human workers) plugged in or planted into the soil (systems and processes) that help them exceed expectations and produce at a very high rate.

II

LEADERS WHO SEE THEIR ORGANIZATION AS A MACHINE AND RECOGNIZE THAT SYSTEMS AND PROCESSES SHOULD BE CREATED TO SUPPORT THEIR HUMAN WORKFORCE CAN CREATE A WORKFORCE THAT FOSTERS MAXIMUM OUTPUT.

IIIIIIIIIIIIIIIIIIIIIIIIIIIIIIIIIIIIIIIIIIIIIIIIIIIIIIIIIIIIIIIIIIIIIIIIIIIIIIIIIIIIIIIIIIIIIIIIIIIIII

Leaders who see their organization as a machine and recognize that systems and processes should be created to support their human workforce can create a workforce that fosters maximum output.

A great example is one of the areas that came under my responsibility as a vice president. The department had customer loss trends for five years in a row. My boss had suggested we look to sell this piece of the company because, he said, it was a money-loser. When it was budget time in my first year and the team projected another loss, I said, "No. I will neither put my name on nor accept another loss in customers."

They argued that I was setting them up for failure if I budgeted for any growth. I saw their point but also knew that another loss would set the department up to be sold—something I didn't want to happen to this team. So finally, we agreed that for the coming year, we would budget flat—no loss or increase of customers.

On my first visit to the location, about eighty employees attended a welcome breakfast for me. It was not the usual corporate catered event; it was homemade food prepared by the employees. These individuals were loyal and dedicated to the company. They took pride in their work and worked hard. As I got to know them, I wanted to do everything in my power to ensure we could continue to provide a long-term, sustainable workplace for them and their families.

I started working closely with the team (moving the seed from the surface to underground, creating engagement and retention). They had the largest number of business development employees in the state and yet no growth. They had spent years gathering data, data, and more data. The entire team, including the field employees, knew more than anyone about why they were losing customers. They knew more than anyone I have ever talked to about the sales side of the business and how to get the customers back.

They knew everything but did not feel empowered to do anything about it.

As I communicated and invested time with the team on the frontline, I worked cross-functionally with my boss, other departments, and necessary support groups in the corporate and division offices (getting moisture to the seed). I removed some unnecessary systems and processes that were blocking their ability to put into action what they knew was the remedy to this customer loss (removed the choking of the seed). I instituted a training and development plan for the sales team to create confidence and spark creativity for growth.

The team created and formalized a plan, engaged the entire workforce, and built a machine that could succeed around the team. It turned a sea of choppy water—of individuals all trying independently—into one massive tsunami. We went flat in year one (meaning there was no loss). In year two, we gained a couple of hundred customers. In year three, we grew over 2 percent of the total customer base for their area, and we continued growing from there.

My boss later told me this was one of the greatest things I did as vice president. But I didn't do it—the workers did. I simply aligned systems, processes, and people as illustrated in the Parable of the Sower, so the company could yield a hundred times more than what was sown. I spent time with the team, used fluid communication, created constructive abrasion, simplified the systems, and made a couple of process tweaks to empower the workers, so they could do their jobs. As a result, that sector of the company continues to grow and innovate because the seed is no longer on the path, stuck in the rocks lacking communication, nor is it choked by thorns. It's placed in the rich soil where it's able to grow and produce.

By structuring your systems and processes with the Parable of the Sower in mind, you will outpace your competition; adapt quickly to consumer demands; attract, develop, engage, and retain top talent; reduce overhead; increase profits; grow your customer base; and remain relevant in the marketplace, yielding a crop a hundred times more than what was sown.

CHAPTER 7

ALIGNING YOUR VALUES WITH THE ORGANIZATION'S

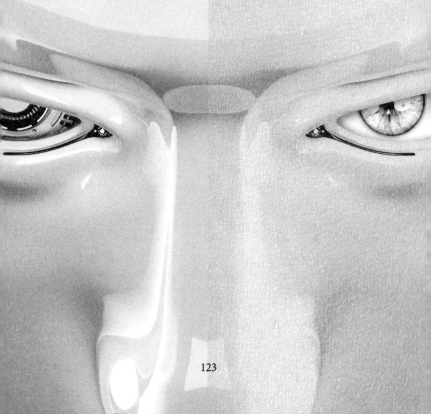

THE

BEST

ROBOT

WINS

J ust as systems and processes facilitate retention and engagement, they should also provide a road map for workplace ethics and values. You can't afford to leave ethics to chance in your organization. When dealing with human workers, you're dealing with a variety of individuals with a wide range of experiences and ideas of what is right and what is wrong. Value alignment is critical.

Every human comes with a unique value set based on individual experiences. Regardless of the personal beliefs of your employees, their ability to completely align with the desired corporate culture is vital for a unified vision and customer experience. It's important to clearly display the values, train the values, integrate the values, and talk about the values until they are woven into the very fiber of the organization. To accomplish this, it's not unusual for companies to create training programs like Hamburger University at McDonald's or the culture book created by the late Tony Hsieh.

Workplace ethics and company values are comprised of more than simply posting messages and slogans on the wall at your business. As we learned in the Parable of the Sower, you need good seed and rich soil. The leader is responsible for choosing the right seed and creating the rich soil they need to grow in.

Leaders fail when they don't follow their own rules. An estimated 35-42 percent of employees witness unethical behavior at work. When words and actions are not congruent, people often defer to the actions. This means that if a leader says one thing and does another, employees are more likely to model what they see over what they hear. More is caught than taught.

Years ago, I was in a meeting with peer executives and two higher-ranking executives. Because of a company-wide reorganization, a group of managers was being retitled "supervisors." It was a title reclassification only and would not change compensation or responsibilities. Still, we recognized that it would impact the morale of the employees and their influence in the community.

The affected employees had the title of community affairs manager, but because they did not directly supervise employees, they could no longer hold a manager title in the new organizational structure. The highest-ranking executives in the meeting suggested that we give those employees business cards with the title of "manager" for their external business affairs in the community, although their internal title would be changed to supervisor.

I asked, "How does that fit into our core values? It seems very disingenuous." Disregarding the dissent in the room, the two upper-level executives took the request to corporate communications and payroll and compensation to get the phony business cards made up. They were told no.

They shouldn't have asked in the first place. Actually, they shouldn't have even suggested it. While it was legal, it certainly wasn't ethical. The company wanted them to act as managers in the community. Shouldn't their title line up internally and externally? That's a small example of how ethical fading starts and creates a culture of unethical business practices over time.

Let's imagine that the company went through with the phony business cards. What seeds would have been planted in the organization? Could this deception have been a path to other ethical issues?

Business cards and titles may seem like a small thing, but it's the small things that can erode your workplace values over time. When you don't pull weeds from the garden, they eventually grow and choke out the desired plants.

As employees advance and move into leadership positions, they will become disenfranchised if they don't see congruence between talk and action among the organization's executives. Once the veil is lifted and workers don't see the top leaders walking the talk for values and ethics, ethical erosion will begin and trickle down to the frontline worker.

The Danger of Unrealistic Pressure

Pressure to perform in an organization can challenge ethics. In your efforts to motivate high performance, you may be creating unethical and unsafe practices in your organization.

I remember telling my team of directors, who were responsible for roughly four hundred employees working on natural gas pipelines, that we had to cut overtime and get the same amount of work done in fewer hours. In the regulated utility business, rates are set based on a snapshot of your business. If you give raises or expenses increase once the rates are set, you have to go in for another rate case to get rate relief. Holding expenses or finding ways to reduce operations and maintenance is part of the game.

We were running at about a 7 percent overtime ratio. My directors wanted to know how they were supposed to get all the work done. My response was, "You tell me." At the time, I thought I was challenging my leaders to get creative, problem-solve, and produce at a higher level. Today, I understand that I created a pressure to perform that had potentially grave and undesirable outcomes by creating unintended consequences and workplace stress as it put the safety of the people and organization in jeopardy.

You can almost see the pressure point when things start going south and ethical fading occurs. Freezing weather, a failed O-ring, and the need to launch by a deadline worked together to cause the 1986 Challenger disaster. A similar pressure to perform created the Schlitterbahn Waterpark case resulting in an indictment and charges against park executives and designers of the Verruckt water slide. Taller than Niagara Falls, the thrill ride was a popular attraction in Kansas City. Even though I was bruised after I rode it with my family, I trusted that Schlitterbahn had built a safe ride. But it hadn't. In 2016, a ten-year-old boy died on the slide. It was a tragedy that was entirely preventable. It is an unfortunate case study of how a culture rich in communication fostering a solid, ethical framework that supersedes pressure to perform could have changed the outcome of this heartbreaking story. If confrontation would not have prevented the child's death, a whistleblower may have. This ties back to communication and why a leader must welcome creative abrasion and make it safe to communicate.

The list of corporate ethical breakdowns is long—Enron, Madoff, Fyre Festival, Goldman, Volkswagen, and more. Often, pressure to perform is a significant driver.

In the Boeing MAX 737 case, longtime customer American Airlines was near making a deal with Airbus, and Boeing rushed to avoid losing a customer. It resulted in nearly 350 people dying, CEO job loss, and a $4.9 billion payout.

A Wells Fargo employee told me that employees would be assigned unrealistic goals every day and the supervisors handing them out knew there was no way they could hit those numbers. Employees figured out all kinds of creative ways to produce the results management was demanding. Many used keeping their jobs as justification for how they did it. My anonymous source told me she never felt right about opening unauthorized accounts and she eventually got fired. The ultimate price tag for Wells Fargo was well over the $3 billion settlement because it included terminations and erosion of consumer trust.

With each ethical breakdown, a trend or a common theme tends to creep into the equation without fail. It's not, "Oh, I didn't mean to do that." If it were, we'd never read about these cases because they would be corrected and go away. The big ones all seem to fall into a pattern of pressure to succeed with fuzzy lines or rules of engagement.

I fell victim to that mindset early in my career during a United Way campaign where the company matched each person's individual donations. We also did group fundraising to increase our numbers. The goal was to be the top area in the company with the highest number of contributions as well as bring in the most money for a great cause. Since the company matched the individual contributions, when we did group fundraising, we thought it would only make sense to link up the individuals who donated to the additional fundraisers to double their contribution. Because some of the donations were small, we couldn't match every dollar back to the exact person, and it created more trouble and questions than good for the campaign. Unfortunately, what was intended to be helpful to the campaign led to some people challenging my intent—and my intent did not match my overall impact. This is why I named my company Intent and Impact with the tagline "delivering the impact your intentions deserve."

I learned that while operating under intense pressure to perform without clear rules, I put myself in a position to have my ethics and values tested and questioned. It's vital for leaders to pressure-test their ethics ahead of time through coursework, constant review, simulations, mentorships, communication methods, and more. By doing this, leaders and individuals can avoid ethical erosion over the pressure to perform.

IT'S VITAL FOR LEADERS TO PRESSURE-TEST THEIR ETHICS AHEAD OF TIME THROUGH COURSEWORK, CONSTANT REVIEW, SIMULATIONS, MENTORSHIPS, COMMUNICATION METHODS, AND MORE.

Create Value-Aligned Systems

As you work to create the right systems and processes, the systems you create must be value-aligned. Leaders must walk the talk. A solid decision-making process is one of the best ways to slow down and ensure that ethical decision-making is happening in your organization at all levels.

Roy E. Disney put it this way: "When values are clear, decisions are easy."

Research shows the average person makes about two thousand decisions per hour and thirty-five thousand choices per day. Decisions are being made every second in your business. The right decisions can boost your stock, while the wrong decisions can assassinate your career and company.

Take Volkswagen, for example. Countless managers and executives knew about the emission cheating software, and their poor decisions lead to criminal charges, civil penalties, plummeting stock, loss of customers, elimination of jobs, and more. While sound decisions can amplify a company, like breakfast all day at McDonald's, bad decisions can be costly.

The closure of iconic Toys "R" Us provides a different kind of example. CBS Business Analyst Jill Schlesinger said it best, calling it "a convergence of bad timing and bad decisions." Retail has been redefined, and the business landscape is brutal. Top-level decisions are not the only ones that are costly to an organization.

One very costly decision made by frontline workers was when United Airlines employees decided to drag Dr. Dao off flight 3411. The flight was oversold, and they needed to make room on the aircraft. They made an announcement asking people to give up their seats voluntarily for a small financial reward. The gate agents were limited in the amount they could offer. When no one took the offer and abandoned their seat, they were left without any other good alternatives and a lack of ability to assess the alternative of what might happen if nobody gave up their seat. Dr. Dao was violently dragged off the aircraft, during which he suffered severe physical pain and embarrassment. This was a costly mistake for the airline and a perfect example of the pressure to perform under a poor decision-making process without clear guidelines for success.

Mistakes and achievements are both a result of your decisions. Solid, consistent decision-making builds a culture of trust in organizations. Jerry West said it well: "If people don't know what to expect from you as a leader, they will stop looking to you for leadership."

ETHICAL LEADERSHIP IS MORE THAN JUST SLOGANS; IT'S WALKING THE TALK.

Ethical leadership is more than just slogans; it's walking the talk. Company leaders must be prepared to make solid ethical decisions and create fail-proof systems and processes for human workers to succeed. For example, expense report fraud costs US companies $1.9 billion annually. Companies that utilize artificial intelligence programs for tracking expenses reduce waste and fraud in their organizations and set their employees up for success. We know the price of turnover, so by reducing terminations and eliminating ethical erosion, you can increase employee engagement and ultimately set your human workforce up for success.

Contemporary management author team Gareth Jones and Jennifer George provide a six-step decision-making process that can help you when making big and small decisions.

I recommend prayer as a part of the decision-making process. With each step, add prayer and ask for insight and wisdom when making decisions. Seeking godly insight and wisdom is a way to multiply the impact of the decision-making process.

~

Here are the six steps Jones and George recommend, along with my comments.

1) **Recognize the need for a decision.** Remember that no decision is, in fact, a decision. Businesses today cannot afford to be stagnant.
2) **Generate alternatives.** Do not succumb to groupthink. Instead, get a diverse group together to brainstorm—the more ideas from various stakeholders, the better.
3) **Assess the alternatives.** Practice "if this then that" (IFTTT). Do some careful forecasting and review for legal, ethical, economic, and practical impact.
4) **Choose among the alternatives.** Rank the alternatives. Identify completeness of information and any potential unintended consequences. This will help alleviate cognitive bias.
5) **Implement the chosen alternative.** Communicate throughout the enterprise. Formalize change management plans, assign roles for implementation and accountability, empower with sufficient resources, and, finally, take action.

6) **Learn from feedback.** This is one of the most critical steps to growth: learning and making necessary tweaks or changes along the way. This step will help you improve on future decisions.

You're already making thousands of decisions per day, so practice this decision-making process until it becomes second nature to you. Improving your ability to make great decisions that align with your values will help you in all aspects of your professional and personal lives and enhance overall workplace ethics for your entire organization.

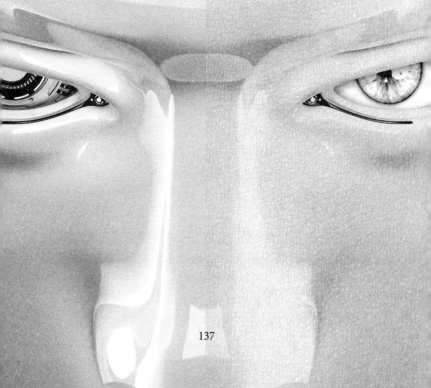

CHAPTER 8

THE COLLABORATIVE AND COLLECTIVE POWER OF PEOPLE

THE

BEST

ROBOT

WINS

T hroughout Jesus' life and ministry, He would use parables to help simplify the spiritual message He was attempting to convey. Jesus told just under fifty parables consisting of moral and spiritual lessons that can be applied to life and business.

The Parable of the Talents was quite a journey for me. However, once I fully grasped the deeper meaning behind the parable, it illuminated a powerful message that, if applied correctly, can give your business a competitive advantage that cannot be duplicated.

> *"For the kingdom of heaven is like a man traveling to a far country, who called his own servants and delivered his goods to them. And to one he gave five talents, to another two, and to another one, to each according to his own ability; and immediately he went on a journey. Then he who had received the five talents went and traded with them, and made another five talents. And likewise he who had received two gained two more also. But he who had received one went and dug in the ground, and hid his lord's money. After a*

long time the lord of those servants came and settled accounts with them.

"So he who had received five talents came and brought five other talents, saying, 'Lord, you delivered to me five talents; look, I have gained five more talents besides them.' His lord said to him, 'Well done, good and faithful servant; you were faithful over a few things, I will make you ruler over many things. Enter into the joy of your lord.' He also who had received two talents came and said, 'Lord, you delivered to me two talents; look, I have gained two more talents besides them.' His lord said to him, 'Well done, good and faithful servant; you have been faithful over a few things, I will make you ruler over many things. Enter into the joy of your lord.'

"Then he who had received the one talent came and said, 'Lord, I knew you to be a hard man, reaping where you have not sown, and gathering where you have not scattered seed. And I was afraid, and went and hid your talent in the ground. Look, there you have what is yours.'

"But his lord answered and said to him, 'You wicked and lazy servant, you knew that I reap where I have *not sown, and gather where I have not scattered seed. So you ought to have deposited my money with the bankers, and at my coming I would have received back my own with interest. Therefore take the talent from him, and give it to him who has ten talents.*

'For to everyone who has, more will be given, and he will have abundance; but from him who does not have, even what he has will be taken away. And cast the unprofitable servant into the outer darkness. There will be weeping and gnashing of teeth.'"
—*Matthew 25:14-30 (NKJV)*

The overarching message of this parable is that each person is uniquely and wonderfully made with distinctive gifts, skill sets, experiences, and abilities. It took me a while to understand that and apply the message of this parable to my life. I used to think this parable was strictly about money, and the talents it talked about were currency. I thought I was supposed to use my skills to double my money like the servants in the parable.

When I left the gas company, I wanted to use my treasure (money) to purchase a business and create wealth. I looked at a number of business opportunities, conducted my due diligence, and concluded none of them were right for me. It seemed like every door was closing. I didn't realize at the time what God was doing. Looking back, I see that He was preparing me for my next assignment and, equally important, preparing my next assignment for me.

Though it wasn't the first time I'd read this parable, God brought it to my attention during a very difficult time in my life. I was at my father's bedside as he was dying. It's an honor to be with someone when the Lord calls them home, and I was blessed to be with my father as he took his last breath on Earth.

Several days later, I sat in the front row at my father's graveside service. I saw the huge hole in the ground, the large pile of dirt beside it, my father's casket, and many people standing around as they prepared to plant him, like a seed in the ground. I thought about this parable, about the gifts and talents, and about my father as he was being buried.

As the children sang, "This little light of mine, I'm going to let it shine," this scripture came to mind:

> *You are the light of the world. A city that is set on a hill cannot be hidden. Nor do they light a lamp and put it under a basket, but on a lampstand, and it gives light to all who are in the house. Let your light so shine before men, that they may see your good works and glorify your Father in heaven.*
> *—Matthew 5:14-16 (NKJV)*

What happens when our light on earth goes out? What have we left behind?

Even though my father's earthy assignment ended, his light was shining through the seeds he planted. My dad was a teacher, counselor, and coach for multiple generations at the same school. The stories that people shared at his memorial service were not about the school system, they were about how my dad touched the lives of his students and their families. Person after person talked about the impact Mr. Horyna had on them as youngsters and how that impacted them today. He has three children, all of whom are making an impact in the world, each with their own children, which creates a legacy impact. My father's life in a town of three hundred people illustrates the compounding power of one person. This lesson cannot be overlooked.

Though my father's earthly body is buried, his treasure continues to multiply.

Treasure used as an illustration in this parable is not referring to money. It's experience, giftings, uniqueness, passion, and individual makeup. It's an inherent and acquired diversity mix that's unique to each person.

Though funerals are primarily a time for honoring and celebrating the deceased, they are also a time when we tend to reflect on and take stock of our own lives. During my father's final days and in the period immediately following his death, I remembered the many parts of my own journey. Thinking about my achievements, my stumbles, and my successes, all unique to me, I realized I'm no better or worse than anyone, I'm just different. My experiences are different.

I have a heart for people, a mind and instincts for business, and a passion for serving God. God gave me a particular set of experiences, lessons, education, and opportunities, so I could invest them in specific ways. This is what the treasure in the parable illustrates.

Leaning into that knowledge, immediately upon returning from my father's funeral, I began my next life and career assignment with the US and Central Florida Christian Chambers. How I was to multiply my "talents" soon became abundantly clear.

How can you multiply your "talents"? The workforce is filled with individuals, each with their own unique set of experiences and giftings. Each person working in your organization has gifts, skill sets, abilities, and talents to pour into their passions. If they are cultivated correctly, your organization can and will benefit.

||||||||||||||||||||||||||||||||||||||||||||||||||||||||||||||||||||||||||||||||||||||||||||||||||

EACH PERSON WORKING IN YOUR ORGANIZATION HAS GIFTS, SKILL SETS, ABILITIES, AND TALENTS TO POUR INTO THEIR PASSIONS.

||||||||||||||||||||||||||||||||||||||||||||||||||||||||||||||||||||||||||||||||||||||||||||||||||

People Determine Your Organization's Potential

As I said, the people who shared wonderful stories about my dad at his funeral didn't praise the local school system, they praised my father—the man, the teacher, counselor, and coach. When people reflect on their time working in your company, they won't be thinking about the number of widgets they made, if they hit their goals every month, or even the profits they helped generate. Instead, they'll be thinking about the people they spent time with, bosses, mentors, coworkers, peers, subordinates, and even their customers.

Workplace turnover—both voluntary and involuntary—is a fact of life in business. Involuntary turnover is when an organization asks the employee to leave; voluntary turnover is when an employee chooses to leave by resigning or retiring. It's important to understand that, outside of retirement, people typically don't leave companies, they leave people.

The machine, systems, and processes that combine to create your business are important, but your business cannot function without people.

When I was laughed at for encouraging investment in people, I tried to visualize the pipeline operating 100 percent on its own without human beings. I couldn't because it's not possible. When you look at the operating budgets of most organizations, the number one expense is typically labor costs. It's not uncommon to see this number at around 70 percent of total business expenses. While we know that 85 percent of job success comes from well-developed people skills, employers are moving their dollars toward technology upgrades, artificial intelligence, and marketing and away from developing their greatest resource, their people.

People determine the potential in your organization. That's why you should hire for personality and train for skill. Get good people and teach them what to do. There's gold within the people in your organization. You just have to be willing to look for it, find it, and help them develop it. Your competitors can copy your product, your menu, or your service, but they can't duplicate your people, your culture, and your ability to empower great people to work in alignment with their calling, passion, and purpose for their lives.

||||||||||||||||||||||||||||||||||||||||||||||||||||||||||||||||||||||||||||||||||||||||||||||||||||||||||

PEOPLE DETERMINE THE POTENTIAL IN YOUR ORGANIZATION.

||||||||||||||||||||||||||||||||||||||||||||||||||||||||||||||||||||||||||||||||||||||||||||||||||||||||||

The talents in the parable are comprised of inherent and acquired diversity traits that exist within each person in the organization. Another way to explain it is the uniqueness of each of the human beings working in your organization. Inherent diversity traits are what you were born with (the way you look, personality style, and preferences). Acquired diversity traits are what you have gained along the way (education, experiences, and societal conditioning). These things combined make up the unique interworkings of the human elements of your business. Because humans are so different, you can't just find any human to fill a spot and have it be a success. You have to understand behavioral science about what motivates each person, provide training and development of individuals, and develop a strong business culture that carries out the mission and purpose of the organization.

I am often asked how I was so successful in my career, and my response has remained the same: I am not that good, but what I am good at is picking the right people. As I've shared in previous chapters, I take time to get to know the workforce—the players and their stories. In doing so, I'm able to surround myself with people much smarter, more talented, and more diverse than I. Yet bringing so many different personalities and unique skill sets to the table can create chaos if not properly managed with vision and leadership. I like to say that managed diversity can produce creative abrasion, which is priceless in the workplace. Tapping into the complex value that the human mind brings into the workplace is key to gaining an advantage over the competition.

Diversity should be more than just a metric in your organization; it must be an integral part of culture and business. Having a strategic universal diversity mindset will result in multiplying your talents. Companies that have a more diverse workforce yield 19 percent higher returns than companies with less diversity. More diversity on a team equates to increased innovation, greater problem-solving, a better ability to serve a unique and different customer segment, and improved employee relations.

We are all uniquely and individually made. We are the masterpiece of our creator. "For we are God's masterpiece. He has created us anew in Christ Jesus, so we can do the good things he planned for us long ago" (Ephesians 2:10, NLT).

While unique due to inherent and acquired characteristics, scientific literature tells us that people have recognized and tried to classify personality traits since Hippocrates. Personality and behavioral patterns exist within people, and behavioral science proves there are patterns in behavior. The better you are at recognizing patterns of behavior, the more successful you can be at putting the right team together. As I explained in Chapter 2, people are more task- or people-oriented. The behavioral science model laid out in DISC has two more quadrants that task-oriented and people-oriented individuals fall into: active and passive. Active-oriented individuals make decisions fast with very little information needed. Passive-oriented individuals make decisions slowly with a lot of information and time to ponder all of the facts needed.

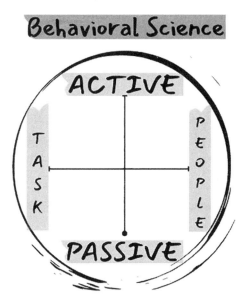

Having these two personality types in the workplace can create friction. People who like to give a lot of detail feel that the active decision-makers are not hearing them. Individuals who don't like a lot of information when making decisions feel interrogated by those that need more information.

Once, as a consultant, I was hired to help a board deal with an "ankle biter" board member. The term they used for the board member immediately told me this individual was causing them grief and pushing back on initiatives in the boardroom. So the first thing I did was a DISC behavior profile for the entire board. That helped me quickly understand what the issue was.

The entire board profiled as active decision-makers with one outlier, the "ankle biter." When I explained the situation, the board was able to see that having an entire leadership team made up of quick, decisive decision-makers that needed little to no detail put the company at risk of moving too quickly. The value the slower decision-maker brought helped mitigate risk. It forced everyone to examine the details and slow down the decision-making process to ensure decisions were sound and didn't fall into the "flavor of the month" management philosophy.

The board finally understood the value the "ankle biter" brought to the team and agreed to slow down long enough to answer questions, identify new strategies, and analyze information. They even agreed to find more board members who enjoyed analytics and details and who weren't shy about asking a lot of clarifying questions to eliminate groupthink and generate creative abrasion on the team. When the perspective changed, frustration was replaced with acceptance, which then turned into valuable conversations and initiatives for the organization. This diversity mix created some beneficial constructive abrasion at the board level.

As the vice president in Texas, I recognized that my director team profiled heavily on the strategy and task side of the business with a mix of active and passive decision-makers. My top leadership team which was driving employee and customer interaction was better equipped to deal with numbers than humans. One of the leaders reporting directly to me was not a director but profiled heavily on the people side and had a behavioral style that mirrored a majority of the workforce and population. His role was in public relations and communications, and he was the only one in my direct leadership team that profiled as an S, representing steady, loyal, great listener, in tune with the workforce. This style makes up approximately 30 percent of the world's population. I invited him to attend our leadership meetings to ensure that, while we were hard-driving leaders, we never left the human element out of the strategy or focus. This paid off big time.

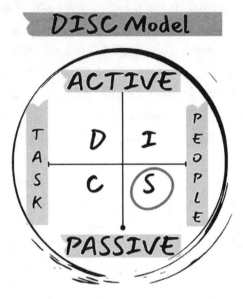

When a major winter storm seriously impacted the El Paso operations, rolling brownouts and blackouts, plus all the related chaos that comes with extreme cold and ice, meant everyone in the company was working around the clock. The pressure was tremendous. The public relations manager slept in our emergency operations center, so he could give regular updates to the public.

This emergency lasted three days. When it was over, we congratulated ourselves on a job well done and got some much-needed sleep. After we were back on our regular schedule, the public relations manager came to me and said, "These employees sacrificed so much for us to be successful. Without them, this whole thing would have been a huge disaster and a major black eye for our company. I think we need to show our appreciation for all they did and let them know how much we recognize them for their efforts."

He was right. So we put on one of the greatest appreciation parties for our team that I can remember. We had images of the storm and our employees working scrolling on the video monitors. We had balloons, music, and a buffet of the best local cuisine. All the directors and I stayed for the entire event, shaking hands and thanking each person individually for his or her contribution and efforts. Having this recognition party improved relationships and strengthened the team's culture, and created loyalty and engagement at all levels. But it wouldn't have happened had I not developed a diverse leadership team.

To grow others, you have to fully know and understand the unique gift and skill set you bring to the organization, so you can identify the unique skills and talents you need to surround yourself with. Unfortunately, it's not uncommon for leaders to put people who look and behave like themselves on a team, which reduces the inherent and acquired diversity mix on the team and results in lower returns.

Consciously seek diversity on your team. Identify patterns of behavior, so you can surround yourself with task- and people-oriented leaders who are active and process-oriented decision-makers. John Maxwell talks about the law of the lid in his book, *21 Irrefutable Laws of Leadership*. The law of the lid shows us that people follow leaders that have a higher leadership level than they do. If you are the lid for your team or organization, it makes sense to constantly grow yourself, so you can grow others. Remember, hire for personality and train for skill. Skills can be learned, but personality is inherent and the first line of diversity in an organization.

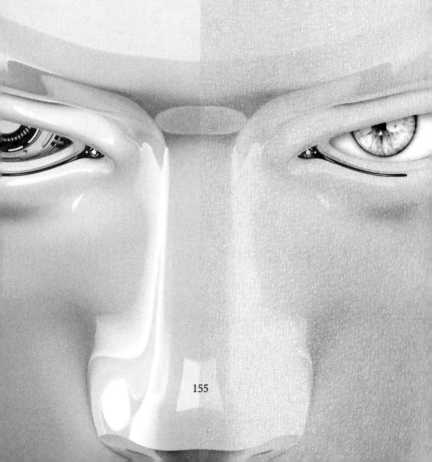

CHAPTER 9

LET THE HUMANS
BE HUMAN

THE

BEST

ROBOT

WINS

ow does the Parable of the Talents apply to your business? Let's take a look at four clear lessons.

"For the kingdom of heaven is like a man traveling to a far country, who called his own servants and delivered his goods to them. And to one he gave five talents, to another two, and to another one, to each according to his own ability; and immediately he went on a journey.

"Then he who had received the five talents went and traded with them, and made another five talents. And likewise he who had received two gained two more also. After a long time the lord of those servants came and settled accounts with them.

"So he who had received five talents came and brought five other talents, saying, 'Lord, you delivered to me five talents; look, I have gained five more talents besides them.' His lord said to him, 'Well done, good and faithful servant; you were faithful over a few things, I

will make you ruler over many things. Enter into the joy of your lord.' He also who had received two talents came and said, 'Lord, you delivered to me two talents; look, I have gained two more talents besides them.' His lord said to him, 'Well done, good and faithful servant; you have been faithful over a few things, I will make you ruler over many things. Enter into the joy of your lord.'" —Matthew 25:14-22 (NKJV)

Lesson 1: Identify the Right People for the Right Roles

Get the right people in the right roles so they—and your company—can flourish. Based on how the master gave out the talents, he could yield a total of fifteen talents. If he gave five talents to the one that buried the treasure and one talent to the one that doubled the five, his return would have been eleven. But he gave the right amount of treasure to the right people.

The master in this parable gave the talents to each according to his own ability. This could easily be the job you entrust to your employees every day. The key in this is that each was given according to their ability. This is why it's vital that you fully know and understand the requirements for each position and have a thorough understanding of how that fits into the greater organization to accomplish the mission. Once you understand that, know your human capital, so you can hire for personality and train for skill. When people know they are valued, their ideas are welcomed, and you see their potential even when they might not, they will meet and often exceed your expectations.

||||||||||||||||||||||||||||||||||||||||||||||||||||||||||||||||||||||||||||||||||||||||||||||||||||||||||||||||||||||

WHEN PEOPLE KNOW THEY ARE VALUED, THEIR IDEAS ARE WELCOMED, AND YOU SEE THEIR POTENTIAL EVEN WHEN THEY MIGHT NOT, THEY WILL MEET AND OFTEN EXCEED YOUR EXPECTATIONS.

||||||||||||||||||||||||||||||||||||||||||||||||||||||||||||||||||||||||||||||||||||||||||||||||||||||||||||||||||||||

My career is a perfect example of this. Early on, someone saw something special in me. I was in my role as a director for about nine months when I got called to the president's office. It was fifty miles from my office and, as I made the drive, every decision I ever made was going through my head. What could I have done that was worth a command appearance in the president's office?

The drive seemed interminable. Once at the division office, I got on the elevator and could feel my heartbeat quickening as each floor passed. When I stepped off the elevator, the president's assistant was waiting for me with a smile and asked me to sit in the waiting area for what felt like forever. I was finally called into the office where my boss and the president were looking quite stern. The president said, "Do you know why we called you in here today?"

I'm sure they could see the fear on my face as I said no. Then they started laughing. These two were pranksters, and I should have known they were up to something. They wanted to tell me in person that they'd put my name in for an executive role in the company.

I had only been a director for nine months, and I could not believe they thought I was ready for that next step and that I would do a good job, but they did. We see it in the Bible time and time again: God doesn't call the qualified; He qualifies the called. We are told in 1 Samuel 16:7 (NIV), "The Lord does not look at the things people look at. People look at the outward appearance, but the Lord looks at the heart."

A great example is King David. He was passed over by his own father to be the king, but God called him out and the Spirit of the Lord came powerfully upon him. He later went on to slay a giant trained in combat with just a slingshot and a stone. When they tried to put the soldier's armor on the young David, he was awkward and unable to go forward in it. He recognized that he was best equipped to slay the giant with just five smooth stones from the stream and his shepherd's bag and the sling in his hand.

You have Davids in your organization. They are filled with the gifts, talents, and abilities to help you take your business to the next level. Look deep within your organization, identify the unique gifts that each person brings to the job, and align that with their ability. That's where the gold lies.

God uses people to accomplish His mission. So run your business the way God runs His kingdom. The Bible has so many stories about people who were called to do great things. These people are in your organization. They have the ideas; they are filled with the gold you need to take your product, your business, your idea to the next level.

Let's fast forward to when, as a vice president at the gas company, I was responsible for nearly four hundred employees. One person reached out to my assistant, requesting a meeting with me. I checked with the director she worked under; he told me they were preparing the documentation to terminate her for unsatisfactory performance.

She arrived in my office with a desperate look on her face. I invited her to sit at the conference table and gave her 100 percent of my attention. She pulled out a notebook filled with pages and pages of documentation about her job—the requests, inconsistencies, frustrating experiences, and imperfections. As she talked, I saw her unique giftings. She was a dedicated employee, she loved the company, she loved working for the company, she was a genius with details, processes, numbers, and correctness—but she was miserable in her role, and her job was miserable with her. Her detail and task orientation were impeccable, but her lack of people skills had her working in a place that was not at all in her strength zone.

Instead of terminating her, we reskilled her. We moved her to a different department and put her in a job that helped pull out her passion for details. She went from the verge of being fired to flourishing because we were able to identify the right role for her. She stayed there for years and then got a huge opportunity to build on that same job role and skill set at a much higher level within the organization and eventually in another company with even higher authority.

Matching the right person with the right position, whether you have two or twenty thousand, whether you are managing employees or volunteers, is critical to your success. As a consumer, have you ever spoken with a customer service agent who clearly should never speak with customers? Or worked with an accountant who had multiple errors in your reporting? It's not that these people are necessarily poor employees, it's that they're likely in the wrong roles. When you clearly define the position and create alignment with the overarching mission and goals of the organization, you can then identify the right person for that role and empower them according to their ability.

Lesson 2: Invest in Your Human Workers

Just as the master invested his talents with each servant, you must invest time, training, coaching, and professional development in your workforce. Once you have your processes and systems in place and have aligned the right person for the right role, you have the opportunity to grow your competitive advantage even more through investment in your human capital.

Many managers focus on the employee output and forget about their responsibility to input for greater output. That input comes in the form of development. Not only will developing your workforce create a qualified workforce that is better equipped to serve your customer, it will also increase employee retention and decrease overhead. Workers want to grow and develop in their roles. They want to see a career path and know there is a plan for their development and future. Surveys show that 90-95 percent of employees say that they would stay at a company longer if it simply invested in helping them learn.

Millions of dollars are lost each year due to a lack of soft skill development in the workplace. Upskilling is taking your human capital and growing it. You aren't adding more overhead or more people; you're simply helping your workforce learn more and work better with others.

Imagine if the time you deal with employee issues could be reduced, and you could have your workforce focused on the mission daily. Let's say you have one hundred workers working eight hours a day with all eight hours applied to moving the mission forward—that's eight hundred mission-critical hours. But if you have 20 percent of your workforce involved in a conflict or issue, either internally or externally with rework or even customer complaints, you have reduced the number of mission-critical hours being worked in your organization. That means you have to add overhead to get the job done. Communication, empathy, tolerance for differences, and coaching are examples of ways to upskill your organization. Soft skill development uses people to create a competitive advantage.

It's essential to recognize the need for reskilling and upskilling in your organization. Human workers are going to need to be reskilled as artificial intelligence is introduced in the workplace. You may have a great employee who is dedicated to the mission and is a proven asset, team player, and natural leader, but you make a sound business decision to replace that person's job with AI. Do you want to lose this asset and hire an unknown who might be qualified to do the new and more advanced job you need with the introduction of AI? Or would you rather retain the human you already have and grow their knowledge by reskilling them? Reskilling and upskilling existing workers cost far less than turnover and add compounding value to the organization.

RESKILLING AND UPSKILLING EXISTING WORKERS COST FAR LESS THAN TURNOVER AND ADD COMPOUNDING VALUE TO THE ORGANIZATION.

This is where and how the best robot wins!

A great example of this is Amazon, which states on its website: "We know that a strong culture and active investment in our people allows us to attract the diverse, innovative employees we need to understand and exceed our customers' expectations today and into the future." The company has made a $700 million commitment to pilot, launch, and scale training programs for one hundred thousand employees by 2025.

Invest in your people just as the master did with his servants. You can do this through tuition reimbursement, onsite training programs, mentoring programs, coaching, leadership and development courses, continuous process improvement courses, and more. The investment in training and development will help you attract, retain, and engage top talent as you improve service levels to external and internal customers, strengthen the organizational culture, improve the overall talent pipeline, produce upward mobility for employees, create loyalty and cultural alignment, and provide job security and safety to innovate.

Lesson 3: Empower Your People

Once the master gave the talents to the three servants according to their ability, the passage says he "immediately went on a journey." Notice it did not say he left and got his binoculars and watched his servants to see what they were going to do with the talents. No, he invested the talents according to their ability and immediately left. It goes on to say that after a long time, the master came back.

Several lessons can be learned from this point in the parable. The master empowered his servants and left for a long time; he did not expect immediate results. Create the systems and processes, get the right people in the right roles, and let your people pour in their passion.

For many years at Arizona Diamondback games, Derrick Moore, aka the Lemonade Guy, could be heard chanting, "Lemonade, lemonade like Grandma made." With an infectious smile and a boisterous voice, Derrick was as popular as the Diamondbacks. The people voted this lovable icon as Major League Baseball's top vendor in 2015. Not only was this an honor for Derrick, it was great publicity and thousands of dollars of free marketing for the team.

It happened because Derrick understood that his job was to sell lemonade at the games and poured his personality and passion into becoming a staple at the games.

In 2021, Derrick came down with a rare illness. He had no insurance, and his family set up a GoFundMe account to raise $50,000 for his medical bills. Months after sharing the page, Derrick's family raised over $135,000. If Derrick had not been genuinely engaged, if he had just followed the rules and delivered lemonade while hating his job every step of the way, he would not have been named Vendor of the Year and created a great return for the Diamondbacks. More important, his family wouldn't have been able to nearly triple the donations needed for his medical expenses. Derrick understood the systems and processes for the job and was empowered to pour his unique skill set into the role. That not only helped the company he worked for, it may have saved his life.

The best way to empower people is to set expectations and rely on your measurements. You must have systems and controls in place to help manage and enrich performance. Inspect what you expect, but in the end, empower people to do their jobs.

In the absence of systems and processes, managers tend to micromanage. Effective measurement will support the employees by providing purpose for their jobs, reinforcing alignment to the mission, helping measure organizational slack, and freeing up the leader to work on more complex problems. Helping your team understand the goals and expectations will help them feel empowered with the freedom to succeed.

The system to successful empowerment is:

1) Get the right systems and processes in place.
2) Clearly define the position and show alignment with the overarching mission and goals of the organization.
3) Identify the right people for roles based on their giftings and unique abilities.
4) Invest in those people by providing training and development opportunities for them.
5) Allow some time for the development to evolve. (Bloom where you are planted.)
6) Empower your people to do their jobs, and get out of their way.

Having the proper measurements are critical. You get what you measure.

Here is a perfect example: I was retained to fix a "get what you measure problem" for an organization. Company X, a customer contact center, wanted to keep talk time low for the call center employees. The company believed low talk time would allow them to take more calls and answer more calls with less staff, saving the company money.

They began measuring talk time, coaching talk time, posting agent results of talk time on the walls, and holding employees accountable. The person with the lowest talk time was treated with great regard and rewards; the person with the highest talk time was in the beginning stages of disciplinary action (up to and including termination).

The customer service agents rallied and gave Company X leadership precisely what they were asking for: low talk time. The leadership team was slapping high-fives at the water cooler because reduced talk time meant the ability to answer more calls without adding additional staff. Unfortunately, they only measured talk time. The problem was that they didn't think about the unintended outcomes of an unbalanced system of measurement.

Within a month, there was a significant spike in incoming calls. Quality of calls declined (there is a cost to poor quality). Issues weren't resolved and customers had to call back (generating more calls the company was not staffed to take, which resulted in mandatory overtime). Customers were frustrated and dissatisfied. The billing department was slammed with rework (creating overtime in that department). Call center agents were having to talk with angry, upset customers (impacting morale). Company X got what it wanted and was measuring—and it was a nightmare.

An effective control system should measure the right things. Key performance indicators (KPIs) trickle down to create the measurements and controls. Remember, you get what you measure, so measurements and controls must be thought through and balanced to provide the desired outcome through a balanced scorecard that flows to each employee having individual performance measures and goals. Goals should be specific, measurable, accurate, relevant, and timely (SMART) and be flexible enough to respond to unexpected events.

The accuracy of controls provides leaders with the ability to reward, recognize, and correct employee behavior. It also allows for the ability to monitor and predict organizational performance. Timeliness of the controls supports the ability to respond to leading indicators instead of failure due to lagging indicators. In the absence of controls, leaders tend to micromanage employees and change processes without measuring the impact of the change or desired result. Controls with empowerment are harmonious and allow your employees to have the freedom to assert their unique personality and style into their roles, like the Lemonade Guy.

As you empower your people to do their jobs, encourage them to identify problems. Help them see the value they bring and empower them to solve problems when they have the opportunity and ability to do so. The problems the top leaders are solving should be the most complex issues that can't be solved on the front line, such as problems that require policy or process changes to correct. Encourage your human talent to communicate the problems they are not able to solve so that your leadership team is only dealing with complex issues and not minor encumbrances. By focusing on the larger issues, you can be a better steward of your limited time and lean into your unique ability to solve complex issues.

As your workforce becomes problem-seers and -solvers, top leaders must listen more than they talk. Remember, the recirculation pump takes time, energy, and effort. The answers every leader needs to be successful, innovative, adaptable, and agile for your consumer lie within your organization's people.

Loren Gary, former associate director at Harvard's Center for Public Leadership, said: "The ability to identify the most important problems and devising imaginative responses to them is crucial to superior performance in the modern workplace, where workers at all levels of the organization are called upon to think critically, take ownership of problems, and make real-time decisions."

Solving problems requires you to think enterprise across the lines of all departments.

Lesson 4: Recognize Great Performance

Learn to tap into the power of intrinsic motion and recognition. In the parable, the master came back, and each of the servants gave an account of his investments. For those who returned a profit, the master was pleased and gave praise: "His lord said to him, 'Well done, good and faithful servant; you were faithful over a few things, I will make you ruler over many things. Enter into the joy of your lord'" (Matthew 25:23, NKJV).

Tapping into what motivates people is a combination of art and science. Having clear and concise metrics that trigger reward is the value of objective measurements. Subjective and spontaneous recognition can also help to extract great performance and incite intrinsic motivators. What the master said to his servant in the parable can be translated in contemporary business as a promotion or more responsibility; however, recognition doesn't necessarily mean more money or greater power.

Intrinsic motivation in the workplace is when a person is inspired by the enjoyment, purpose, growth, and passion of the job. Extrinsic motivators are raises, bonuses, and other forms of compensation. When employees are aligned with their purpose and passion, the culture is one of intrinsic motivation, which is a greater driver of performance than extrinsic motivators.

Let's look at Maslow's hierarchy of needs. You can't reach self-actualization, which is the desire to become the most you can be, if steps one through four haven't been met. However, the ability to reach step five rests in a person's internal desire to become the best they can be.

Here's how this model plays out in the workplace:

1) Physiological needs are met by making a living wage, putting food on the table, and meeting basic needs.
2) Safety needs are met through steady, secure employment in a physically safe environment, not worrying every day that the job will be taken away or they will be fired.
3) Love and belonging needs are met through a sense of connection to the company and mission (the right people in the right position).
4) Esteem or confidence is met through a person's ability to perform the job, the empowerment to do a great job, and recognition of a job well done.
5) Self-actualization can be met when the first four needs are met.

The point is there is very little correlation between job satisfaction and salary.

Consider this: 70 percent of leaders think they are motivating and inspiring. Yet, a Forbes survey found that 65 percent of employees would forgo (yes, I mean pass up voluntarily) a pay raise if it meant seeing their leader fired. Remember, people don't leave companies, they leave people.

If you want to motivate employees, pick the right people for the job. Help those individuals align their purpose and passion with the role they play in the organization and show them how that ties into the organization's overall mission. Set the right controls in place to measure success, offer development, and empower them to do their job, and the intrinsic motivators will drive excellent performance. Put processes and systems in place to help identify problems along the way and recognize great performance. People will work harder for praises than they do for raises.

Let's consider an example of what can happen when these tools are not applied.

One day as I was working in my home office, the silence was interrupted by screams from a man. I went to my back window, where I saw six dirty, sweltering landscapers being berated by the apparent boss, who was on top of the tractor mower. They were installing plants and sod around a new home. It was mid-summer in Florida. The unforgiving sun was blazing, there were no trees for shade, and the work was physical and grueling.

The man on the mower was yelling at the top of his lungs. Even through my closed window, I could hear most of his words. He called the workers lazy and a few other choice words I won't repeat here. He said he would fire them all if they didn't get back to work. It was noontime and scorching hot. I watched as the workers, all with their heads and shoulders slumped over, reluctantly went back to their respective duties. The boss sat comfortably on his perch, obviously quite proud of himself for getting these "lazy" workers back on track. After about five minutes, he drove away, maybe to another job, or maybe to an air-conditioned vehicle or restaurant.

Curious about what would happen next, I continued watching. One by one, the workers gathered on the side of the house where there was a little shade. With their backs resting against the wall, sitting in the cool dirt, they took out their lunches and bottles of water. They ate and drank, talking and laughing with each other. I couldn't hear what they were saying—after all, they weren't screaming—but I imagine they were laughing at the boss who didn't know they weren't working. I laughed with them and went back to work.

I was curious about how the job would progress, so I glanced out the window from time to time. From my vantage point, I could see the boss coming back. I shot up from my desk and ran to the window to warn them. I'm not sure how I would have gotten their attention, but my efforts weren't necessary. They heard the tractor. In unison, they jumped up as if there were a fire under their pants. Each one grabbed their respective tools and took their positions as though they'd never stopped working. As the tractor came around the corner, all the boss saw were six landscapers working diligently under the blistering sun. I could almost see his chest puff out in pride as if to say, "Look at what a great boss I am!"

But, of course, he wasn't a great boss. People are not motivated to do a great job for your company because you yell at them, insult them, and demand that they do things. That leadership style only results in less work and more problems for management to deal with. Imagine how much more could have been accomplished if the boss understood Maslow's hierarchy of needs as applicable to motivation along with many of the other tools we've discussed.

We get to see a little of that negative leadership behavior as we see the story unfold for the servant that merely buried the one talent he received in the ground.

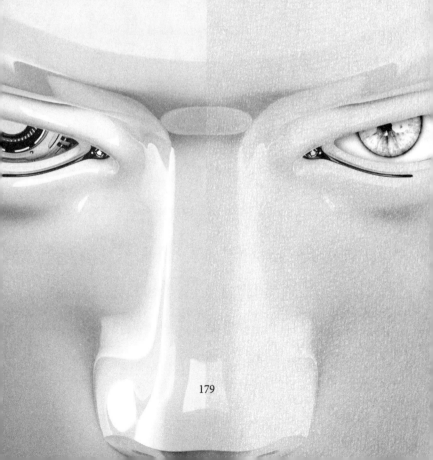

CHAPTER 10

ELIMINATE FEAR

THE

BEST

ROBOT

WINS

s the parable moves on, we can learn a number of lessons about creating an environment for human workers from the servant who buried the treasure.

"Then he who had received the one talent came and said, 'Lord, I knew you to be a hard man, reaping where you have not sown, and gathering where you have not scattered seed. And I was afraid, and went and hid your talent in the ground. Look, there you have what is yours.'

"But his lord answered and said to him, 'You wicked and lazy servant, you knew that I reap where I have not sown, and gather where I have not scattered seed. So you ought to have deposited my money with the bankers, and at my coming I would have received back my own with interest. Therefore take the talent from him, and give it to him who has ten talents.

'For to everyone who has, more will be given, and he will have abundance; but from him who does not

have, even what he has will be taken away. And
cast the unprofitable servant into the outer dark-
ness. There will be weeping and gnashing of teeth."
—Matthew 25:18-30 (NKJV)

The master gave according to the servants' ability. The talents were clearly on loan; they did not belong to the servants. From what I can tell from the passage, there was no instruction on what to do with the talents each servant received. The servant that was given one buried the talent clearly out of fear and his perception of the master.

You have human talent in your organization that falls in the same category as the servant trusted with one talent. A manager plays a huge role in creating a work environment that fosters creativity, productivity, and expression—or the opposite. Employees who don't feel safe will have a fear response in the workplace and never move past step one on Maslow's hierarchy of needs. Derrick Moore, the Lemonade Guy, was empowered to do his job, and he did it exceptionally well. But a fear response from him might have had him walking with the lemonade tray, barely speaking, and just waiting for people in the stands to raise their hands and ask to purchase a refreshing drink.

Managers creating a fear response in the workplace might cause employees to bury their gifts, talents, and abilities. To survive and blend in, they will only do enough to get by without drawing any attention to themselves. Creativity, innovation, adaptability, and great service don't rise to the surface in an organization where employees are fearful.

||||||||||||||||||||||||||||||||||||||||||||||||||||||||||||||||||||||||||||||||||||||||||||||||||||||||||||||||||

CREATIVITY, INNOVATION, ADAPTABILITY, AND GREAT SERVICE DON'T RISE TO THE SURFACE IN AN ORGANIZATION WHERE EMPLOYEES ARE FEARFUL.

||||||||||||||||||||||||||||||||||||||||||||||||||||||||||||||||||||||||||||||||||||||||||||||||||||||||||||||||||

Leaders create a fear space by micromanaging, criticizing, threatening, creating too many controls and processes, being risk-averse, and shutting down any new ideas. I remember flying five hours round-trip on the company plane with my boss and mentor to make a business improvement pitch to a male in a power position. After we pitched, he leaned back in his chair and threw his snakeskin cowboy boots on his desk. Then, looking over his glasses, in a firm and authoritative voice, he said, "I am going to give you two gals enough rope to hang yourself with."

I don't remember exactly what my boss said in response to this aggressive, fear-inducing behavior, but she wasn't flustered and she was smiling when we walked out of his office. While it appeared that we were making a pitch, she had already received the approvals necessary from her boss to move forward with this change. The visit was an attempt to get buy-in from the corporate office, communicate the changes, and garner support. While he had power in his position, she had control in her wisdom.

We laughed all the way home about his reaction to her refusal to even acknowledge his blusterous behavior. His boots-on-the-desk, disrespectful attitude was a tactic he used to create fear and intimidation and hold back our efforts to innovate, adapt, and change the status quo. It was at that moment I understood how fear could stifle creativity in the workplace, but I wasn't prepared for how it might impact me on a larger scale.

Less than a year after I became the vice president in West Texas, a business decision was made to file a rate case. I was sent to a weeklong rate school and told to negotiate the case in the most contentious regulatory environment in the company's area of operation.

While on paper I was the one negotiating the case, in reality, I had little to no authority to negotiate in a way that would result in a settlement. Remember when David went to fight Goliath, they tried to put a soldier's armor on him. It was bulky and weighed him down. He quickly shook off the armor and entered into battle with the tools he knew he would win with.

Not only was I not allowed to negotiate the case the best way possible for the area, I was highly micromanaged by my bosses, who had little to no intel into the best strategies for success. After a long nine-hour publicized hearing, I was ready to make my remarks. I had been told by the division and corporate office they would be watching. I was exhausted, scripted (which I don't do well), handcuffed, and ready to be utterly embarrassed by the appointed board. I was so mentally unprepared, ill-equipped, frustrated, and terrified about saying the wrong thing I could feel my knees shaking behind the lectern. While I had on pointed high heel shoes, I could sense my toes shaking. Thoughts swirled through my mind: *Do I have any color in my face? Will my voice shake like my body? What am I doing here? I hate my job!*

I would have given anything to bury my one talent in the dirt and quit!

I did not want to suffer the consequences of this flogging from the board, from the quarrelsome city attorney, from my legal team, from the newspapers, from the community, from my team of directors, from my boss, and from corporate. I stood at the lectern thinking if I could just say something to thread the needle between my "script" and the truth, it might work—or get me fired.

The room was silent. All eyes were on me. Lights, camera action! I turned on my smile and opened my shaking lips to speak—and you won't believe what happened next. The fire alarm in City Hall went off, and the building was evacuated. The ten-hour day ended with a fire alarm that was a Hail Mary from the Lord. They never figured out why the fire alarm went off, but in my spirit, I understood and thanked God for that save.

The next step of this debacle was a vote by the city council. I mustered a few words and they immediately and unanimously voted to decline the increase. That meant we would go on appeal to the Texas Railroad Commission—an even bigger stage, higher price tag for the ratepayers, and more time spent on this project. As I walked away from the lectern, having experienced the most public rejection I have ever received, the lump in my throat was so big that I felt as though someone had just karate chopped me right in the neck. I'd been rejected before, but not in such a public forum, in front of the city council, the news media, the live streaming into our corporate and division offices, and in front of my team.

One city council member walked up to me and said, "I am so disappointed in your company." Another followed with, "You disgust me."

I was disgusted, too, but not by my company. I was disgusted by my inability to execute the plan I intuitively knew would have worked—an inability driven by fear. If I had been able to communicate the company's message, the need for recovery, the great corporate citizenship in the community, the amazing jobs we created, and explain it in a way that made sense, the way I needed to, we would not have been spat at for trying to recover our costs of doing business.

While the strategy they told me to use may have made sense to the leaders above me from their division offices in a zip code five hundred miles away, they did not understand the politically practical methodologies of communicating differently with people. To secure approval for the increase, I had to tell our story, and I had not been allowed to do that. I was set up to fail. Worse, fear kept me from trying anything other than what I had been told to do.

Because I was so new to my role, it's possible the top leadership team didn't trust me enough to empower me to do what I instinctively knew I needed to do to negotiate this case. Comparing myself in that situation to the servant who buried the master's talent, I often wonder: *did the servant with the one talent have the same chance at success the other two servants had?*

What type of culture have your leaders established? In a fear-based culture, humans are not embraced, confident, or able to flourish and innovate. They're afraid to tell the truth, speak up, and point out problems. Communication is top-down only. Work is micromanaged, behavior is driven through punishment, and mistakes are met with harsh consequences.

Going back to Maslow's hierarchy of needs, hierarchy number two is safety. Without the ability to feel safe at work, it's nearly impossible for a human worker to move to number three, love and belonging.

In 2012, Google launched Project Aristotle, an initiative to determine factors that matter when creating a successful team. Their findings were published in a *New York Time Magazine* article titled "What Google Learned from its Quest to Build the Perfect Team." Here's what they discovered:

> *What Project Aristotle has taught people within Google is that no one wants to put on a "work face" when they get to the office. No one wants to leave part of their personality and inner life at home. But to be fully present at work, to feel "psychologically safe," we must know that we can be free enough, sometimes, to share the things that scare us without fear of recriminations. We must be able to talk about what is messy or sad, to have hard conversations with colleagues who are driving us crazy.*

Systems and processes are vital for the machine to run, but it's essential that those systems and processes be set up to maximize the value-added benefits that only humans can contribute. Leaders with technical skills are generally far less competent when it comes to leading human workers than those with people skills.

||||||||||||||||||||||||||||||||||||||||||||||||||||||||||||||||||||||||||||||||||||||||||||||||||||

THE DICHOTOMY OF A SUCCESSFUL BUSINESS IS EQUAL PARTS STRATEGY AND EQUAL PARTS LEADERSHIP.

||||||||||||||||||||||||||||||||||||||||||||||||||||||||||||||||||||||||||||||||||||||||||||||||||||

The dichotomy of a successful business is equal parts strategy (systems and process) and equal parts leadership (people). You've heard this before: people don't care how much you know until they know how much you care. And as I said in Chapter 8, people don't leave companies; they leave people. That can be expanded to this: people don't leave companies; they leave people and often bad bosses.

Bad bosses are bad for your health. Workplace stress is a billion-dollar problem in the US Fear-based work environments create workplace stress, and workplace stress can create a significant multiplier to your operating expenses. According to the American Psychological Association cited in *Harvard Business Review,* approximately $550 billion is siphoned off the US economy annually due to workplace stress. Each year, 550 million workdays are lost due to workplace stress. An estimated 80 percent of accidents are attributed to stress. High workplace stress increases voluntary turnover by 50 percent.

Employee engagement is the best predictor of workplace well-being. Studies show that employees prefer workplace well-being over material benefits. We discussed the concept of employee engagement when we examined the Parable of the Sower. Now let's break down the human leadership elements necessary to create a workplace culture that celebrates and emphasizes human strengths and capabilities and extracts maximum employee engagement.

In 2009, senior executives at Google wanted to understand why there was a huge variance of effectiveness within their management team. They recognized that some managers and their teams excelled while others did not. So Google did what Googlers do: they started gathering data to put the scientific data behind what makes a great manager so they could duplicate, hire, and train the right leaders. They called this Project Oxygen. It identified behaviors common among the highest-performing managers. In this order, a high-performing manager:

1) Is a good coach.
2) Empowers team and does not micromanage.
3) Creates an inclusive team environment showing concern for success and well-being.
4) Is productive and results-oriented.

5) Is a good communicator—listens and shares information.

6) Supports career development and discusses performance.

7) Has a clear vision/strategy for the team.

8) Has key technical skills to help advise the team.

9) Collaborates across Google.

10) Is a strong decision-maker.

We have discussed several of these characteristics of leadership that are necessary to create an environment that brings out the absolute best in the human workers, empowering them to become the greatest performing asset the company has. A company's competitive advantage exists in its ability to set up processes and systems to enhance and extract maximum human engagement.

The two servants who doubled their talents likely did well because they were not afraid of the master. It appears he was more familiar with them and their ability because he trusted them with more talents than the servant who buried his talent in fear.

Let's take a deeper look at this parable. The servant who buried the treasure saw the master as a hard man, reaping where he did not sow and gathering where he did not scatter. "I was afraid," the servant said. The other servants did not say this, which leads me to believe that they had more knowledge, face time, and understanding of the master and his way of operating.

This could also be why he gave according to the ability. Perhaps he did not know the ability of the one he gave one talent to, or perhaps the one that received one talent was not at all skilled for this type of assignment. Is it possible the two who doubled the talents were given more initially because they had a better relationship with the master? They communicated with him, they knew the rules and expectations, they were empowered to perform, and they felt safe in the actions they took.

When we look at behavioral science coupled with Maslow's hierarchy of needs, we understand that self-actualization is not achieved without passing through the first four steps (the meeting of physiological needs, safety needs, love and belonging needs, and esteem or confidence). It's likely that the servants in the parable who doubled the talents had reached self-actualization, but the one who buried and returned the talent had not.

This parable teaches us that fear makes people bury their unique gifts. When you eliminate fear and set up an environment that aligns purpose, gifts, and passion with the company's overall mission, you create an opportunity to multiply your employees' talents, gifts, and abilities.

When it Really is Just Business

Even with a great leader, sometimes employees just don't cut it. When I was trying out for the worship team at church with a friend, the music director invited both of us to join the team. My friend said, "Do you take everyone who tries out?"

His response was rich with wisdom. He said, "Absolutely not! If I allowed everyone into the worship team and they are not called to do that, I hold them back from their calling and what they should be doing. I'm not going to get in God's way like that."

The point in sharing this is there are times when you'll have people on your team who aren't aligned with your workplace culture, strategy, company values, or team dynamics. In my career, I have had to terminate upwards of fifty employees and, of those terminations, less than 8 percent were for performance issues. I wrestled with every one of these decisions.

Once my then-four-year-old daughter overheard me discussing the termination of an employee with a director. During her bedtime prayer that night, she began to cry and then sob over the employee she never met. She asked God to help him and his family, to give him food, to help him find a new job. This little girl reminded me that no matter the cause for termination, the act separated the person from the paycheck, the livelihood, the ability to feed his family. In her innocence, my daughter reminded me that I should never be numb to terminations. Each one needed to be thought through completely, each person needed to be given ample opportunity to correct the behavior, and termination should always be a last resort. She reminded me to never remove my heart from the firing process. A business must run, a business must return a profit, and a business may need to make some difficult decisions to survive, but the human element should always be recognized and considered.

While the master in the parable went about it in the wrong way and was likely responsible for the underperforming servant, he was right to let him go. The key is to combine compassion with respect and practicality. As the leader of an organization, you have a large sphere of influence and responsibility to your employees, customers, and communities. Utilitarianism is an ethical approach to leadership that should be considered. When you compromise one position for the wrong person or turn away from a need to terminate someone or reduce the workforce, you, in essence, are sacrificing the success of the entire mission for one person.

I applied for a president's position in a company that once had its stock trading around $45 a share. At the time of my application, the stock was down to the $2.50 range. I knew the business model had great potential to make a strong resurgence with the right systems, processes, and people. In my twenty-fifth—yes, my *twenty-fifth*—interview at the corporate headquarters, I asked a question: "What has been your focus for training and reskilling the leadership team?"

The response was that the CEO had cut all training to afford to retain the entire workforce. The CEO didn't want to let anyone go. This CEO was likely on the people side of the dichotomy with little to no understanding of strategy.

I explained that sometimes there is a need to eliminate positions. If your production needs are down and declining but your staffing remains constant, you are, in essence, sitting on overhead you do not need. The solution is to communicate the mission and strategy, reskill and upskill the top talent, make reductions where necessary, and unify the remaining workers through innovation and collaboration. By recentering the business model, unifying employee engagement, and eliminating bureaucracy, the company might survive. I flew home a day later, feeling like I nailed that final interview, only to be told, "We feel you create too big of a risk for our organization."

While I was disappointed, there was no weeping and gnashing of teeth. I thanked them for the opportunity and realized immediately I dodged a huge bullet. A short time after I went through this process, the CEO resigned from the company. With a new CEO in place, the stock has nearly doubled over two years.

When top management could not sufficiently put personal feelings aside to ensure the business was healthy, I knew they were a people-oriented leadership team with little to no understanding of the need for task and strategy. While people are hugely important in the success of an organization, a balance must be struck with structure and strategy to maximize the yield. It was evident I was not a good fit for the organization, nor would my ideas be welcome or appreciated. After all, for leaders and workers alike, just as there needs to be a balance between processes and people, one must understand in the end, it ain't personal, it's just business.

CHAPTER 11

REHUMANIZING
YOUR
WORKFORCE

THE

BEST

ROBOT

WINS

T he information I've shared in this book is a combination of practical business experience and technical knowledge. I went from being a college dropout stocking shelves in a truck parts store to being named the youngest executive in a Fortune 200 company. I transitioned from delivering gas to delivering JD Powers award-winning customer service to more than 2.1 million customers across three states in the Midwest. I received an undergrad in psychology, a master's in marketing, and a senior executive leadership certification from Harvard Business School with an emphasis in innovation, globalization, and leadership diversity.

I started my own company to help leaders and boards navigate the business labyrinth and deliver the impact their intentions deserved. I became a college professor teaching courses in management, ethics, leadership, organizational behavior, entrepreneurial vision and strategy, and managing cultural diversity. Ultimately, when I was able to layer more than twenty-five years of field experience on top of teaching, it clarified the concept of building a business like a machine.

When I took over the Central Florida Christian Chamber of Commerce and launched the U.S. Christian Chamber of Commerce, I didn't have people, processes, or systems. I was running my company, teaching at the university, and being a mom when I bit off the challenge of re-engineering the Christian Chamber model. Then, one evening, while out for a walk to clear my head, I realized that to do it all, I was going to have to become a robot—meaning I would need to standardize as much as I could, add AI where possible, shore up my weaknesses with people stronger than me, get very disciplined in my schedule to stay healthy and work efficiently, and ultimately build a machine.

When I look back on my life and career, I understand the factors that contributed to my success: fail quickly and adapt fast, surround myself with great mentors and leaders, and strike a balance between strategy and leadership.

KNOW YOURSELF SO YOU CAN SURROUND YOURSELF WITH PEOPLE THAT POSSESS STRENGTHS THAT ARE YOUR WEAKNESSES. YOU ALONE ARE NOT ENOUGH.

Know yourself so you can surround yourself with people that possess strengths that are your weaknesses. You alone are not enough. 1 Corinthians 12:14-27 (NIV) explains it perfectly:

> *Even so the body is not made up of one part but of many.*
>
> *Now if the foot should say, "Because I am not a hand, I do not belong to the body," it would not for that reason stop being part of the body. And if the ear should say, "Because I am not an eye, I do not belong to the body," it would not for that reason stop being part of the body. If the whole body were an eye, where would the sense of hearing be? If the whole body were an ear, where would the sense of smell be? But in fact God has placed the parts in the body, every one of them, just as He wanted them to be. If they were all one part, where would the body be? As it is, there are many parts, but one body.*
>
> *The eye cannot say to the hand, "I don't need you!" And the head cannot say to the feet, "I don't need you!" On the contrary, those parts of the body that seem to be weaker are indispensable, and the parts that we think are less honorable we treat with special honor. And the parts that are unpresentable are treated with special*

*modesty, while our presentable parts need no special
treatment. But God has put the body together, giving
greater honor to the parts that lacked it, so that there
should be no division in the body, but that its parts
should have equal concern for each other. If one part
suffers, every part suffers with it; if one part is honored,
every part rejoices with it.*

*Now you are the body of Christ, and each one of you
is a part of it.*

By recognizing the Bible as the best and most useful business book in your library, you can appreciate the inherent value of diverse humans and foster an environment of inclusion. This allows the pendulum to rest in the middle between strategy and leadership.

With an understanding of the collective power of people, processes, and parables, you're ready to maximize your competitive advantage by rehumanizing your workforce.

I challenge you to remember a time in your career and life when someone—a boss, coworker, family member, coach, mentor, or friend—recognized your unique giftings. They believed in you, engaged you, inspired you to become better, and ultimately helped you grow. How did their faith in you make you feel? Did it make you want to work harder? Did it give you new insight into your strengths? Did it empower you to try and do new things?

With that in mind, I encourage you to remember the Golden Rule: "Do to others what you would have them do to you" (Matthew 7:12, NIV). Be that person for someone else.

Now let's briefly consider the opposite scenario. Remember a time when someone dehumanized you and made you feel "less than"?

I recently came across a situation that grieved my spirit. My source asked to remain anonymous but told me I could share the story. They recently went to work for a Fortune 500 company that employs more than forty thousand human workers. This multibillion dollar organization enjoyed a 900 percent increase in stock price from 2011 to 2021 and is currently trading at over $300 per share.

In one area of the company, humans are responsible for manual labor, moving heavily soiled merchandise from trucks inside the warehouse for cleaning and processing. The company orients new employees with the typical four Ps: password, paperwork, processes, and a project. The employees' first project is to change into their work uniforms and get started.

The work uniform has a name on it—but not the name of the employee wearing it. Employees are given temporary uniforms to wear for at least the first two weeks until their permanent uniforms arrive. Those temporary uniforms belonged to former employees and bore their names. To make it worse, this company provides uniform rentals. It would have been quick and easy to remove the name badge and provide the initial temporary uniform with no name. But they didn't.

This is not how to orient people into a new company and culture. It's humiliating and degrading to require someone to wear a name badge that is not their own name, especially when they're meeting new coworkers and supervisors for the first time. It's even worse when that worker goes home, maybe stops to do a little shopping on the way, and then greets their family wearing a uniform with someone else's name on it. It may seem like a minor thing, but it's not. Remember in Chapter 4, I talked about how important it was to the people who worked in my division that I knew their names? When you tell someone that their name is not important, you're telling them that *they're* not important.

Whether this attitude toward onboarding is an isolated pocket where people are not valued or perhaps a painful indication that the growth has outpaced the initial culture, this practice shows that the company places little to no value on the unique giftings and contributions the human worker will have inside of the machine. In the two months my source has worked at this organization, there has been a 50-percent turnover in this department alone.

Regardless of whether this company is a good place to work in terms of pay and benefits which are set at the corporate level, in the long run, the cost of dehumanizing the human capital at the departmental level will be far graver for the company than it will be on the human workers.

||||||||||||||||||||||||||||||||||||||||||||||||||||||||||||||||||||||||||||||||||||||||||||||||||||||||||||||||||||||||||||||

BUSINESS IS A MACHINE, AND ULTIMATELY THE BEST ROBOT WINS.

||||||||||||||||||||||||||||||||||||||||||||||||||||||||||||||||||||||||||||||||||||||||||||||||||||||||||||||||||||||||||||||

Business is a machine, and ultimately the best robot wins. Your job as a leader is to create the best machine, aligning people, processes, and systems. Vintage management principles of planning, leading, organizing, and control are essential tools for building and operating the machine. Leaders who construct a great machine create alignment for the enterprise's mission, vision, and values, which drive the grand strategy mix (multifaceted approach to strategy within the organization). This grand strategy mix should consist of a comprehensive set of transformation initiatives, a keen understanding of emerging technology, Porter's Five Forces model (competition in the industry; potential of new entrants into the industry; power of suppliers; power of customers; threat of substitute products) to analyze competition and reveal external opportunities and threats to an organization's SWOT analysis.

This mix should also include an in-depth awareness of each of the products' life cycles as well as having a controlled and measurable understanding of each key performance indicator and align that with every position within the organization and then layer that with each customer and market segmentation. The grand strategy mix will help leaders strengthen inefficiencies and identify opportunities to position the machine for success. Leaders creating the best robot have a clear understanding of lean techniques and recognize the importance of continuous process improvement and value re-engineering. Strategy alone is just ink on paper, and even the greatest strategies will fall short if you are not engaging your human capital to execute.

Your competitors can copy your product, your business model, your menu, or your service, but they can't duplicate your people, your culture, and your ability to empower great people to work in alignment with their calling, passion, and purpose for their lives. There are more than seven billion people in the world and a one in sixty-four billion chance that someone has the same fingerprint as you. Coupled with inherent and acquired diversity, it's safe to conclude each human is uniquely made and has the ability to create your organization's competitive advantage.

When you can attract, develop, retain, and engage the right individuals within your organization, a true competitive advantage emerges. Processes and systems should be created to inspire, support, and fuel your human workers. Human capital has the unique advantage of serving, adapting, and growing your customer base in a way that will help you yield a crop a hundred times more than what was sown.

Rehumanizing your workforce will create an environment that unifies strategy and leadership to successfully align people, processes, and systems to create a multiplier effect on your efforts and ultimately "help you gain an unfair advantage over your competition," says Global Sales Guru Joe Pici.

Essential Elements for Rehumanizing Your Workforce

Ready to begin the exciting process of rehumanizing your workforce? Use these essential elements as a guide.

- Conduct leadership assessments using behavioral science, like DISC, EI, and 360 feedback tools as well as a balanced scorecard with measurements designed around employees, customers, and KPIs.
- Assess and map an organization-wide DISC analysis for all employees, including the board of directors.

- Review time, effort, goals, initiatives, and investments to balance each of the vintage management principles. These are nonnegotiable. Every point has a purpose and should be equally represented in the management of an organization.

    1) planning (strategy)

    2) leading (people)

    3) organizing (processes/systems)

    4) control (measurements)

- Listen for and learn your authentic organizational culture and measure the variance between actual and desired. This allows you to attract great talent that is the right fit.

- Be intentional and create a standard onboarding experience to absorb new talent quickly.

- Create programs that engage top talent through empowerment, career enhancement, and collaboration (there is a direct link from employee engagement to your top-line and bottom-line revenues).

- Develop systems to retain top talent by cross-functional development, reskilling, and upskilling (replacement costs are equivalent to six to nine months of an employee's salary—it's more cost-effective to reskill and upskill than replace).

- Understand your customer lifetime value costs and the direct correlation between customer retention and your human workforce, so you can empower them to retain and serve customers.

- Create a culture of collaborative communication and review the results of the communication assessment in Chapter 4 with your leadership team.

- Simplify everything. Cut through bureaucracy. Review every process and system. Understand why policies and procedures exist and how they tie to the overall mission.

- Eliminate redundancy, automate jobs or tasks when possible, and keep each position fluid and nimble as the organization adapts and evolves.

- Set people up for success by offering clear guidelines for ethical performance (when the values are clear, decisions are easy; inspect what you expect).

- Eliminate ethical fading by removing unachievable and unrealistic pressure to perform.

- Use ethical simulations to teach leaders a solid decision-making process that is fully encapsulated in prayer and reflection.

- Set up a system that allows you to connect the dots between the position and person. Find a perfect match that aligns their passion and purpose with their role in the company.

- Consciously seek individuals with three inherent and three acquired diversity characteristics to create two-dimensional diversity within the organization (companies with more diverse teams yield 19 percent higher returns).

- Create balanced measurements and develop a system as explained in Chapter 9 to fully empower people and incentivize outstanding performance.
- Use Maslow's hierarchy of needs to help trigger intrinsic motivators for the team and recognize outstanding performance.
- Create an environment of inclusion by eliminating fear in the organization. Foster a culture rich in recognition and reward versus silence and punishment.
- Address performance and process issues quickly and make difficult business decisions with dignity.

In today's competitive business climate, technology and customer needs are evolving at warp speed. Companies that do not adapt quickly are failing faster than ever before.

To stand the test of time, companies and individuals must adapt and remain agile regardless of the organization's size. Creating a solid business machine that attracts, develops, and retains a high-quality, engaged workforce will multiply profitability for the organization. The elements to rehumanize your workforce provide a glimpse into the areas that you can start to focus your efforts on to construct the best robot.

Your business is a machine. Your job as a leader is to create processes and systems that empower and engage your workforce to create a competitive advantage in the marketplace, so your company will stand the test of time. Businesses will never run without humans, and humans need jobs to create the means for survival. Ultimately the best robot wins, and in the end, it ain't personal, it's just business.

I'm Krystal Parker, and business is my sport!

KRYSTAL PARKER

Intent and Impact

DELIVERING THE IMPACT YOUR INTENTIONS DESERVE

INTENTANDIMPACT.COM
KRYSTALPARKER@INTENTANDIMPACT.COM